COLOSSIANS
A Portrait of Christ

Colossians
A Portrait
of Christ

JAMES·T·DRAPER JR

LIVING STUDIES
Tyndale House Publishers, Inc.
Wheaton, Illinois

Unless otherwise indicated, all Scripture
verses are quoted from *The Living Bible,* copyright
© 1971 by Tyndale House Publishers, and
are used by permission. Other Scripture quotations
are from the King James Version of the Bible (KJV).

First printing, July 1982
Library of Congress Catalog Card Number 82-80621
ISBN 0-8423-0358-8

CONTENTS

1
Grateful Anticipation
Colossians
1:1-8

PERHAPS THE MOST BEAUTIFUL, consistent witness to the person and character of Jesus Christ is given to us in this epistle to the Colossians. The church at Colosse was located about a hundred miles from Ephesus. It is obvious from reading through the epistle that the Apostle Paul had not been to Colosse. That is probably why he went farther in the opening verses to identify himself as an authoritative minister of Christ than he normally did. He did not do that, for instance, in 2 Corinthians.

The church at Colosse was largely a Gentile church. Colosse itself was not a Jewish community as were some of the other places where Paul ministered. False teachers had apparently begun to infiltrate the church. We can only surmise the nature and content of that false teaching. When we look at the Bible, and the New Testament in particular, we are not always sure what questions the writers are answering. If we have only answers and no questions, it can be difficult to determine the subject being discussed.

But we can conclude, from reading Colossians and from the emphases that the Apostle Paul gave, that the false doctrine had largely to do with the character of Jesus Christ. Some were saying that Jesus Christ was not the all-sufficient, adequate Son of the eternal God. There were some who questioned his deity, and some who questioned his humanity. They were saying that he was not all that man needed. The false doctrine had begun to dilute and compromise the pure gospel that had been preached by those who established the church.

This error was marked by several characteristics. One, the church was becoming very *ritualistic*. There is nothing wrong with ritual as long as we understand that ritual is like a telescope—not something to look at, but something to look through. In Colosse, the ritualism showed up in certain religious observances. The false teachings had turned the eyes and pulled the hearts of the people away from a pure and undefiled love for Jesus Christ and had diluted their understanding of his character and person.

Second, the church was becoming *legalistic*. They were concerned with food, drink, and special days. They were being instructed to do many things, some of which were wrong and sinful.

We face the same temptation today to become legalistic. We may feel that if we do certain things, we are good Christians; at the same time, we may not love God. He may not have our hearts at all, yet we may still give the outward appearance of being dedicated because we are doing certain things that have been prescribed for us by others.

The church, through false teaching, was also becoming very *mystical*. It apparently was involved with demonic spirits, for we find Paul talking about *principalities* and *authorities*. Paul used these words elsewhere to describe the demonic world. Apparently some worship of angels was also involved.

We can understand the concern that the Apostle Paul had about the false teachings that were being propagated. There was also a lack of godly conduct among some of the people, as well as a tendency toward impurity, because of the error being spread through the church.

As we carefully read what Paul wrote, we discover that the problems were not yet too severe. Most of the news Paul received from Colosse was good. The church was going well. Most of the people were working hard, worshiping, and loving the Lord, but considering the errors within the fellowship, Paul felt that prevention was the best cure. He dealt with problems before they could get out of control and disrupt the church.

Colosse had a strong, viable church, which was moving ahead for God. But wherever God's people are being responsive and receptive to the Word of God and the mission he has assigned to them, Satan will be working also, as evidenced by the problems within the Colossian church.

The best way to meet error, to meet false doctrine, is to preach the truth. We don't have to know what all the cultists believe in order to witness to them and combat their error. All we need is to know what we believe. The Apostle Paul preached truth to combat error. To be very sure, he contradicted the false teachers, but he did it in the course of preaching the truth. Controversy wins few converts. The way to deal with disorder and heresy is to preach the truth. Paul condemned the false teachers by magnifying Jesus Christ.

Herein lies a beautiful truth: If we believe right about Jesus Christ, we will believe right about everything else. Most of the problems people have with the Word of God are about matters that Jesus didn't think were problems at all. Jesus referred, for instance, to the Mosaic authorship of the Pentateuch. Jesus believed that Moses wrote it. If we have a low view of Jesus, we may have questions concerning the Mosaic authorship of the Pentateuch. But if we have a high view of Jesus, we know that if Jesus said it, we can accept it. That solves all the problems. When we start right with Jesus Christ, error will be eliminated. The Apostle Paul's epistle to the Colossians is a beautiful picture of Christ, intended to be the answer to the false teachings in the church.

THE CLEAR ASSIGNMENT

A specific assignment is outlined very clearly in verses 1 and 2. There are three distinct designations. First, Paul called himself an *apostle*. The word "apostle" means more than just an errand boy or a messenger. In the original language it means "one sent out for a purpose, with a mission." It implies that the one sent out has the specific authority and power of the one who sent him. An apostle stands as God's spokesman to the people. It was important for Paul to make this point very clear since he had never been to Colosse: "I wish you could know how much I have struggled in prayer for you and for the church at Laodicea, and for my many other friends who have never known me personally" (Col. 2:1).

Paul established that he was an "apostle of Jesus Christ by the will of God." He was an apostle not because he was a great man, but because of the grace of God, by the will of God, by the choice of God. That is always true. We are saved by grace and we serve by grace. No one serves in a position of authority or responsibility because he or she deserves it or because his or her life merits such a response from God. Rather, it is out of God's grace.

The prophets and the apostles, without exception, claimed to be on a mission for God: "God called me." "God sent me." "I preach because God called me to preach." One could hope that whatever we do vocationally, in the secular world and in the church, we are doing by the will of God.

The letter was from Paul " . . . and brother Timothy." Timothy was a fellow worker. This verse established his clear assignment to this church and his partnership with Timothy.

The letter was "to faithful Christian brothers" ("saints" according to KJV). The word *saint* means a "person set apart for God's purposes." Saints have a unique calling, having been called out of darkness into light. They have been called to declare by their lives and their witness the "unsearchable riches" of God. All of God's people have a clear assignment. They are saints, set apart for the purposes of God, saved, and commissioned to serve him.

Paul called them "faithful Christian brothers in the city of Colosse." There is the hint of a warning here. He said he was addressing the saints and the faithful brothers. The phrase could be understood: "Some of you might not be faithful. I want to be sure I am talking to the faithful ones, to those who are standing true." He did not condemn any of them, but he seemed to be warning all of them.

Paul used one of the most strategic and beautiful phrases in the entire Word of God—"... in Christ" (KJV). A Christian may be in Euless or Sacramento or Topeka, but he is always in Christ. He or she lives in two spheres, a citizen of two worlds. Wherever the Christian may be in this world, he or she is still in Christ.

We are citizens of two worlds. We have allegiances here and we do our jobs here. We do not take lightly our earthly duties and responsibilities, but we are also citizens of a heavenly nation. The Christian's joy and peace are not determined by the circumstances of the physical world. The Christian will do his or her job because it is done in the Lord and for the Lord. It may not be very attractive or rewarding and the praise may be very limited, but the Christian does it because he or she is in Christ.

Wouldn't it be wonderful if the people where we work knew we were *in Christ?* On Mars Hill at Athens, Paul said, "In him [Christ] we live, and move, and have our being" (Acts 17:28, KJV). That should be the testimony of every Christian. We represent Christ if we have him in our hearts.

"Grace be unto you, and peace, from God our Father and the Lord Jesus Christ" (1:2, KJV). Grace is God's undeserved favor toward us. We desperately need grace, but we don't deserve it. "Peace" is more than just prosperity, more than just being blessed. This word carries in it the whole meaning of our salvation. Our sins are forgiven and we are at peace—with God and with ourselves. It all comes through the grace of God.

A CONTINUAL APPRECIATION

"Whenever we pray for you we always begin by giving thanks to God the Father of our Lord Jesus Christ, for we have heard how much you trust the Lord, and how much you love his people" (1:3, 4). The word "always" goes with "thanks," rather than with "praying." The construction in the original language indicates that it might be translated: "We give thanks always to God and the Father of our Lord Jesus Christ, praying for you." Paul was offering continual thanksgiving.

The preposition "for" means "concerning." This word speaks of specific prayer, directness in prayer, boldness in prayer. Paul was saying, "Always, I am giving thanks for you and when I do, I am praying concerning the things that burden you. I am praying by name, specifically for you." The word "praying" here indicates that the person is aware that he is standing face to face with God. What a beautiful witness and testimony! No wonder the first-century church revered, honored, and blessed the Apostle Paul. We cannot love people better than by continually praying for them. If there is someone we have a hard time loving, we should try praying for him. We might be surprised at what takes place.

The faith the Colossians had in Jesus Christ did not just mean that Christ was the object of their faith, though that was true. It meant that their faith derived its strength and vitality from Jesus. He was not only the object of their faith, but also the source of it.

Jesus is also the one who builds our faith. Because we are in Christ, we now have a faith that flows from Jesus Christ. And because of our faith in Jesus Christ, we have love for all the saints. We cannot have the healthy kind of faith Paul was talking about without having love for the brethren. These two necessarily go together.

We are never more like Jesus than when we love each other. Our love for each other is dependent upon our relationship with him. We are neither loving or lovable. Only Jesus is. Only as we abide in him will we have the kind of love that ought to be in our hearts.

A CONSTRUCTIVE ASSURANCE

In verses 5 through 8 Paul wrote about what lay ahead, the hope that was coming, the inheritance that is laid up for believers. It was not just a blind hope or a guess, but a constructive, growing, building hope.

"Since we heard of your faith in Christ Jesus and the love which you have for the saints, for the hope . . ." (1:4, KJV). The words "for the hope" should be translated "because of the hope." This hope is related to the faith and love mentioned earlier. So, because of their hope, their faith and love abounded.

What was the hope? " . . . The hope which is laid up for you in heaven." The word "laid up" in Greek is a compound—a preposition and a verb, meaning "off" or "away from," and "to lie." We have this hope set aside in our behalf, away from us, but awaiting us. Being in the perfect participle form, it means that we have a hope that has already been set aside for us. It is already our possession.

Even though it is in the future when God will call us home and we receive it, it is just as surely ours now since it has already been given to us.

Believing that I am a child of God is not taking a leap into the dark. God's promises are as real as anything in life. When God said, "It will be," it already had been. His promises are just as unchangeable as past history. Promises and prophecies are the history God sees before it takes place. It is not a guess but something sure. Peter talked about our having "an inheritance incorruptible, and undefiled, . . . reserved in heaven" for us (1 Peter 1:4, KJV).

Before the false teachers came in, the Christians in Colosse had heard the truth, and in that truth lay their hope. There is no hope in heresy. False doctrine and error question the promises and the veracity of God and bring despair. Heresy causes people to doubt the sovereignty of God. The truth of the gospel is the pure good news from heaven that gives meaning and purpose to life and eternity.

"Ye heard [it] before in the word of the truth of the gospel; which is come unto you, as it is in all the world; and bringeth forth fruit" (1:5, 6, KJV). Two verbs appear in the original language: "bring forth fruit" and "increase," giving a beautiful description of what the gospel in its purity accomplishes. It bears fruit and it grows. It gives life and it multiplies life. Paul was telling the saints in Colosse that they were living proof of the gospel because it was changing their conduct and their lives and was doing something inside them. It was growing internally and increasing externally. The good news was being spread. That was the assignment God gave the church and we are still at it.

"As it doth also in you, since the day ye heard of it, and knew the grace of God in truth" (1:6, KJV). There is a difference between hearing the truth and committing oneself to the truth. Many people hear the message but never commit themselves to it. Paul took these people back, not necessarily in time to when they first heard the truth, but to the day when they heard it and appropriated it, accepted it.

Some of us may have heard the truth all our lives but have never really grasped it. It has never really "gotten hold of us." Hearing the gospel is more than intellectual assent. It is also receiving its truth into our hearts and lives. It is not enough to be emotionally wound up in a religious experience or to be intellectually fascinated by an eternal truth. One must accept and appropriate it. Truth is not just something to *believe*; it is something to *do*.

"Epaphras, our much-loved fellow worker, was the one who brought you this Good News. He is Jesus Christ's faithful slave, here to help us in your place" (1:7). The construction would indicate that he was not saying, "he is your minister," but "who is for us a faithful minister of Christ." Many scholars believe Paul sent Epaphras the hundred miles from Ephesus to establish the church in Colosse. Later they sent Epaphras back to Paul and he became Paul's minister in a very special way. He was a minister both to the people of Colosse and to Paul, but in the final analysis he was Christ's minister. We may serve each other and minister together, but the ultimate truth is that we are ministers of God through Jesus Christ.

"And he is the one who has told us about the great love for others which the Holy Spirit has given you" (1:8). Some wonder what that statement really means. The word "Spirit" is the Greek word *pneumatos* and the word "love" is *agape*. *Agape* love is a sacrificing kind of love, the love that God produces in us. Epaphras related to Paul the godlike love which the Spirit of God had produced in them.

God's truth is communicated through individuals. Notice that Paul had sent Epaphras with a message, and Epaphras had come back to Paul with a message. The message of the gospel was communicated through individuals. That is the mission God has assigned the church, not just the task of enjoying truth, but of being dispensers of truth. God has made us not custodians but couriers. He has called us not just to protect, but to declare, the truth. The truth is that the gospel does not need defending—it needs proclaiming.

God has said he would honor his Word. We are proclaimers of the truth until God's Son, Jesus, returns. The only reason false doctrine, heresy, and error come is because the church fails to proclaim the gospel in truth.

2

Walking
Worthy of
the Lord
Colossians
1:9-12

PAUL GREETED THE COLOSSIANS, spoke fondly of them, commenting on the good report he had gotten from those who came to tell him of the church's affairs. Verse 9 begins his message to the church at Colosse. By and large the report concerning them was good, but the problems created by false teachers were beginning to erode confidence in the sufficiency and deity of Christ. Along with that had evolved other subtle heresies leading to immorality, unfaithfulness, and dissension within the group.

"So ever since we first heard about you we have kept on praying..." (1:9). Today we sometimes do the opposite. We pray when the report we get is bad, but when it is good, we slack off. But Paul kept on praying even though they were reported to be growing strong and doing the things they should have been doing.

The phrase in the King James Version—"we also"—indicates that they had prayed for Paul. In effect, he was saying, "You are praying for me and I am also praying for you," a picture of the beautiful relationship of God's people. There ought always to be a bond of prayer and the encouragement of prayerful support among God's people.

These four very practical verses, having some very beautiful lessons for contemporary living, are summarized in several key words.

PRAYER

The first key word is *prayer,* in verse 9. The word translated "desire" (KJV) is a word which asks for something specific to be given, not that something be done. It emphasizes the thing asked for and not the person who is doing the asking. The object of this prayer was that God might do something very special.

"I do not cease to pray for you" does not mean that Paul was every moment continually praying. It means rather that he had a habit of praying for them. Invariably there is someone who says, "It is physically impossible to be praying all the time." That would be true if we are talking about specific petitions, but the idea here is of consistent, habitual prayer. There was never a day when the church of Colosse was not in Paul's prayers.

"I desire that ye might be filled with the knowledge of his will" (KJV). The word "filled" means "filled to completeness." Paul wanted them to be filled up to the brim with the knowledge of God's will. The basic purpose of our prayer ought always to be that we might discover and experience the will of God.

Notice "the knowledge of the will of God." Many Greek words could be translated "knowledge." The most common is the word *gnosis.* The false teachers of that time were called Gnostics, a term taken from this word, which reveals their claim to a superior knowledge. But the word translated "knowledge" here is *epignosis.* When the preposition *epi* ("upon" or "above") is added to *gnosis,* the meaning is intensified, taking on the sense of "full knowledge." One cannot have a false full knowledge. We can have a false *gnosis,* but not a false *epignosis.* Paul wanted the church at

Colosse to understand perfectly and completely and to know the will of God. He prayed specifically that God would give them a complete knowledge of his will.

Such knowledge, Paul explained, would "make [them] wise." The word in the Greek for "wise" means the highest form of knowledge. It means to know the principles, the truthfulness, the accuracy of information. It is to be aware of truth. If we had a perfect knowledge of God's will in all wisdom, we would have a perfect grasp and a perfect appropriation of moral understanding. But Paul didn't stop there. He added "about spiritual things." Spiritual understanding is the ability to take knowledge and put it into practice. Many people have all the right answers, yet they live unacceptable lives. They know certain facets of truth but they don't have the ability to incorporate them into their lives. Paul prayed specifically for the Colossians to have this special kind of knowledge.

PLEASE

In verse 10, the key word is "please." As a result of the full knowledge of the will of God, the knowledge that enables us to understand truth and put it into our lives, we will live worthy of the Lord. There could be no higher desire in the heart of any Christian than to live up to his profession. We, who claim to know Jesus Christ, have taken upon ourselves the name of Christ. Jesus Christ was the divine, virgin-born Son of God who gave himself as a sacrifice for us, was resurrected from the dead, and now lives at "the right hand of the Father," interceding in our behalf until he returns to earth again for his people. Paul urged believers to live up to that knowledge.

It is no light thing to be called a Christian. Paul did not pray that we walk worthy of good tradition, or that we be model citizens, conforming to the standards of our society.

He prayed that we would live worthy lives and be pleasing to God. Our goal is to please God, not to get to heaven. We are saved in order to give glory to God. We won't understand what God wants to reveal to us unless we understand it as something to glorify God. We often live unaware of who God is and of what he requires, but if we have the full knowledge Paul was praying for, our lives will be pleasing to the Lord.

This word "live" here means that a thing or person has the value or worth of another. It implies that we need to live as one who has the value and worth of God in our lives. We should live our lives with God's character in our hearts and minds. To live worthy of God means to recognize that as children of God we are part of him and he of us. We are to conduct our lives so that we are continually aware that we bear his name and in that sense, we have his value. "For God took the sinless Christ and poured into him our sins. Then, in exchange, he poured God's goodness into us!" (2 Cor. 5:21). We stand with his righteousness in us. We are clothed in the character and person of Jesus Christ.

Living worthy of the Lord and pleasing God involve "being fruitful in every good work" (1:10, KJV). Doubtless Paul was talking about the work of the Christian. If we bear God's character and his name, then our work will be his work. We are involved in God's purposes of redemption, which is why we still live in a day of grace. It still pleases God to save the lost, to bring souls into his kingdom. If we live worthy of God, we will be fruitful in every good work, and as we do, we will grow and mature in the knowledge of God.

The more we live worthy, the more we are fruitful. The more we are fruitful, the more we are increasing in the knowledge of God. The more we increase in the knowledge of God, the more we are living worthy. On and on the cycle goes as we live in a way that pleases God.

To do that, we need help. It is staggering to think of living a life pleasing to God, and we have to confess that it is not within us to do it. That seed of sin in our nature rebels and struggles against the best interests of our being, against the glory of God. There is something inside of us that wants to draw glory from God, that wants to take and to demand. In ourselves, we cannot live worthy or please God.

POWER

In verse 11, Paul mentioned the power we need to live worthy lives pleasing to God. To the Colossians he said, "We are praying, too, that you will be filled with his mighty, glorious strength so that you can keep going no matter what happens." "Strength" and "mighty" have the same Greek root word: *dunamis,* meaning "power." We brought it into English when one of the most destructive forces in the world was discovered—we called it "dynamite." The words "dynamic" and "dynamo" also come from the same root. It was used in Greek as a noun and a verb in the same context. Paul was saying, "You will be empowered with all power."

Notice that he said we will be strengthened "according to his glorious power" (KJV). He did not say we would be strengthened according to our need. When we have reached the end of what we need, we have not reached the end of what God can supply. The power that God gives us by which to live is not a power to enable us to just get by— that is, proportioned to us on the basis of our immediate need. It is a power given to us on the basis of his ability to supply, according to "his glorious power."

The word for "power" (*kratos*) is used only of God's might or dominion in the New Testament. It speaks of divine power, not psychological gimmicks or emotional upheavals. We are talking about the supernatural, divine power of God coming into our lives to enable us to be what we could never be in ourselves. That is the hope of the church, the hope of God's power blossoming forth in us.

The word "strengthen" (KJV) at the beginning of verse 11 is a present continuous participle. That says that God does not save us and that our lives are to be lived on just the power we got when we received Christ. It suggests that he is continually strengthening us. Day by day he walks with us, guides, directs us. Continually he is empowering us. Whenever the strength is needed, his power is there. It is never based on our need, but always on his supply. Many times we walk faithfully, obediently in him, and he "does exceedingly abundantly" above all that we ask or think. His power is continually evident and present in us.

This divine power is continually producing in us patience and long-suffering (KJV). "Patience" means a steadfast endurance in the face of opposition, temptation, trial, or tragedy. It is the ability to deal triumphantly with anything life can do to us. It is the opposite of despair. God's power in us gives us the ability to meet life head on, so regardless of our aches, disappointments, or changes in direction, God's power can give us triumphant victory.

More than that, this power produces long-suffering, which we need more than we need patience, because long-suffering means victory in our relations with each other. For every one time we have to deal with a circumstance or tragedy, there will be a thousand times we have to deal with individuals. Long-suffering is the ability God gives us to endure insult and injury without retaliation. It refers to patience with people, the ability to be mistreated, to be misjudged, to be condemned, without reacting negatively. God says that as we live worthy of him, as we please him, there is a mighty infusion of his dynamic power daily coming into us that gives us the ability to meet every experience of life victoriously.

Many have a very stoical attitude about problems. They meet adversity with a sense of resigned endurance, but without what Paul added: "with joyfulness" (KJV). We can learn patience and long-suffering, but to practice them *gladly* is another thing. Some of us meet difficulties and disappointments fairly well, but Paul prayed that we would "be filled with his mighty, glorious strength so that you can keep going no matter what happens—always full of the joy of the Lord" (1:11).

God wants to put in us a spirit and a power that are so strong that we will not only be patient and victorious with people who wrong us, but that we may endure with joy. That is the kind of power God gives. Our joy, or lack of it, is an indicator of how we are walking with the Lord. The Christian life should be a joy-filled experience. Such joy can come even when we are doing things we might not want to do. It is one thing to be obedient. It is another thing to be joyful as we obey.

PRAISE

Paul prayed that the Colossians might be " . . . always thankful to the Father who has made us fit to share all the wonderful things that belong to those who live in the kingdom of light" (1:12). To be thankful means to praise him. As God empowers us to be patient and long-suffering—as we walk worthy of him, being fruitful in every good work and increasing in the knowledge of the Lord—we do so with a continual awareness that God is to receive the glory. Having been judged guilty, we are sinners standing before a holy God. But our Father, the judge, has provided redemption for us. If that is not a cause for praise and gratitude, then nothing in all the world is.

We are partners in teamwork with God's people who have been born into the light. Being made "fit to share" does not speak of character, but of privilege and position. We are not worthy, but God in his grace reached down, saved us, and forgave us. That power continually builds into our lives the qualities and characteristics of joyful, glad triumph. We thank God that he has positioned us to partake of all the wonderful things that belong to his kingdom.

3

Redemption
through
His Blood
*Colossians
1:13, 14*

IT WAS THE ANCIENT CUSTOM on occasion that a conquering army would literally take the entire population out of its homeland and put it somewhere else. We read about the Babylonian and Assyrian captivities of Israel and Judah. Once conquered, the people were uprooted and relocated in the land of their new conquerors. It seems fitting that when God conquers us, he delivers us from the power of sin and takes us out of the kingdom of darkness, bringing us into the kingdom of light: "For he has rescued us out of the darkness and gloom of Satan's kingdom and brought us into the kingdom of his dear Son, who bought our freedom with his blood and forgave us all our sins" (1:13, 14).

The key thought in this passage is redemption, which means "to be delivered from the consequences of sin." Three tremendous things happen in our lives when we are set free from sin and its consequences. These three truths are what being saved is all about.

These verses speak about being delivered from the *power* of sin, from the *presence* of sin, and finally from the *penalty* of sin.

DELIVERANCE FROM SIN'S POWER

God has "delivered us from the power of darkness" (KJV). The word "delivered" means "to draw to oneself, to rescue." It is the picture of someone drowning and another coming to lift him out of the waves to save him. Without God, men grope and stumble through life as though walking in darkness, living in the shadows of doubt and ignorance. We are under Satan's power of darkness until God delivers us.

This phrase "power of darkness" appeared already in the New Testament. When the mob came to the garden to capture Jesus in order to put him to death, Jesus asked them why they were so upset. He had been with them and among them many times when they could have taken him. Then he made the statement, "This is your hour and the power of darkness" (Luke 22:53, KJV), meaning it was the hour for them to attempt to eliminate Jesus. Jesus Christ himself faced the power of darkness. Because of his victorious struggle upon the cross and his conquest of death and the grave, he is now able to free us.

Unsaved sinners belong to the power of darkness, of which Satan is ruler. Darkness is not just the absence of light. In this context, and in the New Testament sense, darkness means opposition or hostility to light. "Being in darkness" is not just a condition of being without God; it is being against God. The power of darkness is a realm of opposition to the truth of God. The unsaved sinner who has never known Christ and the forgiveness of sins is in this ungodly domain. When Paul said we are delivered from the power of darkness, he was declaring that we have been delivered from this rebel kingdom and have been brought into a kingdom which is under the sovereignty of its rightful king, Jesus.

The word "power" in Greek is *exousia*, which means "liberty to act," a freedom to express oneself. It has several secondary meanings: "legitimate authority or power" or "a tyranny, a lawlessness, an unrestrained arbitrary power." It is best understood in the latter sense. Being delivered from the power of darkness means being delivered from a kingdom of overbearing, unrestrained, unruly enmity against God and becoming part of the well-ordered, sovereign kingdom of God.

The distinction is important because we need to understand that the power of darkness is a kingdom that is determined to destroy us, a kingdom that works against our best interests. The kingdom of darkness is an unruly, destructive kingdom, which cannot give us anything permanent because it is not itself permanent. It cannot give us anything meaningful because it knows only chaos. It is also tyrannical.

When Jesus died on the cross and shed his blood to redeem us, he delivered us from that chaos and tyranny. The Word of God implanted in us when we are saved will bring wholeness and completeness to our lives. But if we give ourselves to Satan, to the power of darkness, we bring only destruction and despair into our lives.

DELIVERANCE FROM SIN'S PRESENCE

"And brought us into the kingdom of his dear Son" (1:13). "Brought" in this verse means "to transpose" or "to translate." When we transpose something in music, we change it from one key to another key. That is essentially the meaning of the word "here." It speaks of the activity of taking something from one place or state to another. We are transferred, transposed, translated. When we were delivered from the power of darkness and sin, we were transferred into the kingdom of "his dear Son."

Notice it is called "the kingdom of his dear Son." In the original language, that could be translated "the Son of his love." That rich expression indicates to us that the Son is not only the object of his love, but the embodiment of that love, the expression of it. Not only are we translated to a kingdom where Jesus Christ is the object of God's love, but to a kingdom where Jesus Christ *is* God's love.

Thus, we move from the loveless condition of darkness into the realm where God's love is shed upon us. In theology this is what we call *realized eschatology*. *Eschatology* speaks of last things, and *realized eschatology* indicates that those things which lie ahead in a real sense are already here. It means that we have a foretaste of future glory. Heaven lies ahead of us, but we have in the present every assurance that it is ours. It is as surely ours now as it will ever be.

In Ephesians 1, the Holy Spirit is called the "earnest of our inheritance." It is the same word we use as "earnest," or "down payment." If someone buys a house, he may put down what is called *earnest money*, which is part of the down payment, part of the total purchase price. It secures the agreement about the final transaction. In Ephesians 1, Paul was stating that the Holy Spirit is the down payment, the earnest of our inheritance. It means that what lies ahead for the child of God is a present reality in our lives. We have been translated, redeemed, and delivered into the kingdom of the Son of his love.

DELIVERANCE FROM SIN'S PENALTY

We are also delivered from the penalty of sin. "Who bought our freedom with his blood and forgave us all our sins" (1:14). The phrase "bought our freedom" gives us the idea of a ransom payment. In the ancient world, the word "redemption" meant a release effected by the payment of a ransom. It was the word used when a slave was set free. When *we* speak of being redeemed, it means that we have been released from the evil world and the sin that enslaved us and also that our sin is forgiven. Through Jesus Christ we have been delivered from the penalty of sin. We were once slaves of Satan, but now we are free, having been purchased by Jesus Christ, and are now part of his family.

We are purchased "with his blood," Paul wrote. There are those who would have us eliminate references to the blood. Some ask, "Was it necessary for Jesus to shed his blood for us to be saved?" The Bible itself answers, "Without the shedding of blood there is no forgiveness of sins" (Hebrews 9:22). Our redemption came through the shed blood of Jesus Christ. Jesus' death upon Calvary was the act of a holy God, who paid the penalty for human sin. His shed blood satisfied the demands of his holy law.

From the very beginning, man has been shedding blood to cover his sin. When Adam and Eve sinned, blood was shed so that God could provide a covering for their shame. From the Garden of Eden to Jesus Christ's death on the cross, God's way of speaking to the hearts of men and revealing to them his will was through a sacrificial system that required the shedding of blood. The blood was shed, symbolic of the purging of sins. People, in faith, looked forward to the time when Christ would die upon the cross. Every animal slain on a sacrificial altar in Old Testament times was an act of faith looking toward that time when the Lamb, who was "slain from the foundation of the world," would give his life and shed his blood on Calvary. We are redeemed through the shed blood of Jesus Christ.

God could have revealed his love to us in many ways. He could have told us of his love in beautiful stories or poems. He could have demonstrated his love by gracious gifts of beauty and art. But he proved his love to us by shedding his blood on Calvary's cross.

God "forgave us all our sins" (1:14). Just as redemption speaks of a release effected by the payment of a ransom, as with a slave being set free, so the word "forgiveness" speaks of being released from bondage, from imprisonment.

To forgive is thus to release someone from indebtedness. Forgiveness involves the remission of the penalty of our sins which was freely given to us by Jesus Christ.

The word for "sin" here is *hamartia,* which means "to come short of God's demand." When we have done our best, we are still sinners because we come short of God's demand. We do not have the capacity, the strength, the wisdom to be what God wants us to be. Other words are translated "sin" throughout the Word of God, but *hamartia* speaks of our inability to measure up to God's holy demands upon our lives. We are hopelessly in debt to God's righteous justice, hopelessly bound by sin and unable to satisfy the demands of righteousness, integrity, purity, dedication, love, and compassion.

When Paul told us what it means to be lost, he said, " . . . All have sinned, and come short of the glory of God" (Romans 3:23, KJV). He did not say we have come short of man's expectation, of society's average, but "short of the glory of God." Meeting the standard of the glory of God is what God expects of us.

We cannot meet God's demands, however. The only way we can be saved is to admit that we have sinned and failed to measure up to his standard and then to trust him to do what we cannot do, which is to secure our forgiveness.

Blessed possessions are ours! In Christ we are fit for glory. In Christ, we are delivered from the power of darkness. In Christ, we are redeemed and forgiven. It is done! We have been redeemed through his blood, "even the forgiveness of sins." What a ground for rejoicing and praising God!

4

The
Preeminent
Christ
*Colossians
1:15–19*

IT IS SOMETIMES DIFFICULT to divide the thought patterns of
the Apostle Paul as they appear in the original language. He
sometimes goes several paragraphs without a period, as in
the following passage: "Christ is the exact likeness of the
unseen God. He existed before God made anything at all,
and, in fact, Christ himself is the Creator who made everything in heaven and earth, the things we can see and the
things we can't; the spirit world with its kings and king-
doms, its rulers and authorities; all were made by Christ for
his own use and glory. He was before all else began and it
is his power that holds everything together. He is the Head
of the body made up of his people—that is, his church—
which he began; and he is the Leader of all those who arise
from the dead, so that he is first in everything; for God
wanted all of himself to be in his Son" (1:15-19).

The division for this chapter is made arbitrarily, because
the passage logically fits into the verses that precede and
follow it. These five verses are considered separately because they comprise a beautiful picture of the preeminence
of Jesus Christ.

Jesus Christ is the only rightful Lord of creation. He who
set the universe in motion is the one responsible for everything that has appeared or shall appear. No new cosmic

force can surprise him. He knows all about it. He is omnipotent and omniscient. No power anywhere in this world can usurp or take away his sovereignty in the universe.

The Apostle Paul magnified this picture of Jesus Christ to refute the false teaching of the Gnostics at Colosse, who taught that Jesus was not the sole Lord of creation—that he was only one of many emanations from God. The passage before us is a clear picture of the fact that the best way to refute heresy is to proclaim the truth. We need only to know and to declare the truth to refute false teachings, the same way Paul was doing it.

MANIFESTATION

"Christ is the exact likeness of the unseen God. He existed before God made anything at all" (1:15). Because God is spirit, we cannot comprehend him or see him, either with the eyes of our body or of our mind. God cannot be apprehended by natural means. If man were to know what God is like and to understand him, God would have to manifest himself to man. Paul declared that the perfect revelation of God is Jesus Christ. He is the one who revealed God. Paul used two terms to describe this manifestation. First, he said, Jesus Christ is "the exact likeness of the unseen God." The words "exact likeness" mean "representation" or "manifestation." It is true that man is created in the image of God. But we need to understand that Jesus *is* God—the original, perfect likeness of God. The image of God in man is an imperfect one. Jesus is not a copy. He did not become the image of God. He is the image of God, always has been, and always will be. He is the representation, the likeness, the manifestation of God.

This likeness, this representation which we see in Jesus is the image of the "unseen" God. It does not just mean that we can't see God with our eyes but that God cannot be comprehended by unaided reason or intellect. The only way that a man can comprehend God and come into a true understanding of God's character, nature, and person is through Jesus Christ. An incomprehensible God can never be known by human reason or by the capacity of man, but through Jesus, God is made manifest.

It is exciting to realize what God did for us in Jesus Christ. We can understand why Simon Peter said, "Neither is there salvation in any other: for there is none other name under heaven given among men, whereby we must be saved" (Acts 4:12, KJV).

Paul further called Jesus Christ the "firstborn of every creature" (KJV). Some might interpret that to mean that Jesus himself was created, that he is the first created being. That could not be so because the next verse declares that he is the one who created everything. The word that is translated "firstborn" speaks of sovereignty, of rank, of priority. Jesus Christ is not one of many emanations of deity as the Gnostics claimed he was. He is, in fact, the sovereign God himself. It is in Christ that we discover a God who is near. It is in Christ we find out that God cares, hears, pities, and loves us. In Jesus we understand that God saves us. He is the perfect manifestation of God.

CREATION

"For by him were all things created, that are in heaven, and that are in earth, visible and invisible, whether they be thrones, or dominions, or principalities, or powers: all things were created by him, and for him" (1:16, KJV). Regarding creation, Paul was very specific. He didn't leave us to wonder what he was talking about. "By him" should be translated "through him." Through Jesus the creative forces of this world became operative. He is the one who is the agent of creation.

"By him all things were created." It is hard to misunderstand that. No one can believe the Bible and believe in the naturalistic, humanistic explanation of the universe. The Bible declares that all of the creative energies of God were channeled through Jesus. It is a very simple statement. It takes less faith to believe that than to believe the speculations of pseudo-science.

Naturalistic evolution is contrary to everything scientific. It is neither scientific nor intellectual, and yet we are asked to believe it. We can see the extremity to which the man in unbelief will go. When the rich man asked Abraham to let Lazarus return from the dead to witness to his brothers who were lost, Abraham said, "If they won't listen to Moses and the prophets, they won't listen even though someone rises from the dead" (Luke 16:31). The Bible is describing in that simple statement the extremes to which man will go not to believe God. It is difficult to comprehend how set the mind of man is against God. To believe God is not difficult. It is the antagonism of man's sinful heart, not his mind, that refuses to believe God. The Christian faith presents the most rational, logical, reasonable explanation of the origins of everything, but our hearts are set against God so that we prefer to choose a lie rather than the truth.

"By him were all things created, that are in heaven, and that are in earth, visible and invisible, whether they be thrones, or dominions, or principalities, or powers" (KJV).

It is our understanding that the worship of angels, including fallen beings, was a part of Gnostic teaching. Angelic beings and man were worshiped, all of whom were included in this phrase as being created by God through Jesus Christ. Before any of the imagined powers or real powers ever were, Jesus was God's agent in creation.

"All things were created . . . for him." Literally this phrase means that all things were created *unto* him, which tells us that this created universe is moving toward an ultimate goal. It is not a meaningless mass of happenstance, but the moving of a sovereign God in the affairs of man, pointing man towards an inevitable conclusion when all mankind shall bow before him and declare Jesus Lord. All that exists is created by him, and exists for the purpose of giving honor and glory to him. Every relationship of our lives ought to honor Jesus Christ. Every word from our lips and every desire in our hearts ought to give glory to him. Every attitude in our minds ought to be wholesome and healthy and to edify the Body of Christ. The universe has a purpose, for Jesus is not only the agent but also the goal of creation.

FOUNDATION

"He was before all else began and it is his power that holds everything together" (1:17). He is the foundation upon which everything is built. God didn't create everything out of nothing—but by the Son, who was before everything. This indicates a priority in time. Before there was ever any creative act of God, Jesus was there. Personal pronouns in Greek are shown in the inflection of the verb. Here in this phrase, the pronoun is included along with the verb. Instead of simply saying, "He is," Paul wrote, "He, himself is. . . ." Jesus Christ is before all things. He is the foundation of it all.

By him everything "holds together." Jesus is the one who keeps everything from falling apart. We have a skeletal structure to hold our bodies together. Jesus is like that in creation.

We are told that water is composed of two gases, hydrogen and oxygen. Hydrogen is combustible and oxygen supports combustion. Put them together and we have water with which to put out fires.

Suppose for one minute Jesus decided not to hold the

world together and all the water in the world reverted back to its natural state of hydrogen and oxygen. In a split second the world would explode and burn up because it would not be held together. It holds together because he is the foundation upon which it was built.

Jesus Christ is the one who enabled us to put a man on the moon, to send a spaceship to take pictures of Venus, Mars, Jupiter, and Saturn, and to explore the vast expanse of space. As this is true of the created universe, so it is true of all of our lives. The only one who can hold our families together is Jesus. He is the only one who can hold our lives together. We are emotional, volitional, spiritual, and physical people. Only Jesus holds those aspects of ourselves together. Were it not for him, we would fragment and destroy ourselves.

When we begin to fall apart, our only hope is Jesus Christ. There are times when our emotions run away with us, when our anger gets loose, and we become fragmented. The only hope for our fragmentation is Jesus Christ, who holds all things together. If we could understand that, it would put most of the psychiatrists and psychologists out of business. We will never be put together by "all the king's horses and all the king's men." We are put together only by the King by whom everything was created and for whom everything holds together. He is the one foundation upon whom life is built.

PROPITIATION

"[He] is the beginning, the firstborn from the dead; that in all things he might have the preeminence" (1:18, KJV). Jesus, by virtue of his absolute being and perfect divine nature, is Lord of the universe. He is also Lord of the new spiritual creation because of his propitiation, his atoning sacrifice. He became Lord of the Church through his incarnation, death, resurrection, and exaltation at the "right hand of the Father." He was already Lord of the created, natural universe. But when there came into being a new creation, he became the head by his death upon the cross. It is by his death that we are saved. It is the cross that became the focal point of the redemptive purposes of God. Through his death he became the head of the Church.

Christ is the head of the Church, which speaks of an organic relationship. Everything that is good and wholesome in the relationship of a head to a body can be read into this analogy. It is not a perfect analogy in every way, because if the head is severed from the body in any other life form, they both die, and Jesus cannot die. But Christ's headship of the Church speaks of the head's relationship to its body in terms of giving direction and sustaining power. Jesus is the mainspring of the body of Christ, the Church; he is the source of its life, its controlling factor. Just as the head shares itself with the body, so the body shares itself with the head. Jesus Christ shares his life with the Church, and the Church in turn enters into his being and his ministry.

If our churches are to survive, we must function as a body. That does not mean that we agree on everything. For instance, my foot and my hand never agree. My hand is not interested in wearing a sock. There are different functions for each member of the body. Each of us also has unique and individual responsibilities within the body of Christ, but we all agree on Jesus, the head. To him we ascribe praise, glory, and honor. To him we extend our hearts. To him we commit our lives. By him we stand and in his strength we shall serve until he comes.

"Who is the beginning, the firstborn from the dead." Some have disputed this claim, saying that there were other previous resurrections from the dead. But Jesus was the first one to be raised incorruptible, the first one resurrected from the dead who will never die again. He was the only one who was raised with an eternal body. Because he is now in his glorified body, he heads the great host of saints who shall march with glorified bodies at his return into a place prepared for God's children.

"That in all things he might have the preeminence." The word "preeminence" speaks of the totality of the sphere of influence of Jesus Christ. There is no element in this universe outside the sphere of his influence. That is why we praise the Lord Christ. His reconciliation draws heaven and earth together and gives meaning and purpose to all of life.

CONSUMMATION

"For it pleased the Father that in him should all fulness dwell" (KJV). If it pleases God, we ought to be happy with it. We need to understand that the important thing for us is to discover what pleases God. We are so oriented to man. It is the philosophy of our age. When we read "Now is the accepted time; behold now is the day of salvation," we have a tendency to think it means "Now is the time I accept." But the truth is that *now* is the time God accepts. We get saved and get right with God when he gets ready, not before and not after. It is always on his terms and his initiation.

Notice in this verse that Paul didn't say that all of the fullness of God dwells in Christ. In other words, Jesus is not all there is of God. He said "all fulness." Everything that has meaning, value, merit, lasting quality, beauty, attractiveness, loveliness, importance—all dwell in Jesus fully. Whatever we desire dwells completely in Jesus Christ.

God channels our energies in Christ. He regulates and restricts us to free us, to allow us to operate at the highest efficiency. Gasoline is good in our car as long as it is in the gas tank and fuel line. If it gets on the floor or on the engine or in the trunk, it is bad. God channels our opportunities in Christ. In Jesus, all fullness dwells.

The word "fullness" speaks of totality. It means that everything God is in his nature, Jesus is. It pleased God that Jesus was totally, fully, absolutely divine. All divine power resides in Christ.

The word "dwell" is a very specific word in Greek. It means "to dwell permanently," not temporarily. Everything of God, every good thing dwells permanently and eternally in Jesus Christ.

Does he dwell fully in you in your mind, shielding, protecting, and guiding so that you are kept from temptation, depression, and discouragement? Does he dwell in your heart so that your passions and your loves are channeled into his very best for your life? Does he dwell in your body so that you do not abuse it and cheapen it by misuse? In Jesus all fullness dwells. The only way we can know fullness and completeness is in him.

5

Continuing
in the Faith
Colossians
1:20-23

"IT WAS THROUGH WHAT HIS SON DID that God cleared a path for everything to come to him—all things in heaven and on earth—for Christ's death on the cross has made peace with God for all by his blood" (1:20). One of the meanings of the word "peace" is "to bind together." We normally do not think of that as a description of peace. We think of peace as a feeling of calm or tranquility in the midst of turmoil or contentment in the midst of pressure or confusion.

One meaning of the word "peace" is, in fact, "tranquility." But another meaning has to do with reconciliation or cessation of hostility. The use of the word "peace" in the Greek language, as it appears in this context, leads us in that direction. We see the picture of man alienated from God, separated from God by sin. But now, through Jesus Christ, man and God are bound together again, which is what happens when we are saved. At creation, man had fellowship with God. He was bound together with God in perfect fellowship in a beautiful garden that God had created. But man sinned, which removed him from God. Man was no longer bound with God, but separated from him. Whatever else being saved means, it means that our sins are put away and that, in Christ, we are bound together again. Peace has been brought to our souls through the cross.

RECONCILIATION

The means of our being bound together with God was the blood of the cross. When we speak of blood, we are reminded of the Old Testament system whereby the blood of an animal was taken by the priest in a sacrificial ritual. That blood became a symbol of the expiation, the removal of the penalty, of that sin. Man's sin was forgiven in the system of sacrifices prescribed by God through the shedding of blood. When we see the blood of his cross, we are reminded that Jesus Christ was the perfect sacrifice for our sins. His sacrifice on our behalf, his blood, was the means of our reconciliation.

Reconciliation originates with God. We desperately need to be brought back to God, but God is the one who initiates it. "For Christ's death on the cross has made peace with God for all by his blood" (1:20). Reconciliation means that all of the barriers that separate us from God have been removed. There were barriers between man and God. The reconciliation of the cross was necessary to satisfy the removal of the barriers.

Man was a creature of sin, which stood as a barrier between God and man. That barrier had to be removed. But God is holy and could not tolerate sin, and his divine holiness also posed a barrier between God and man. Through the death of Jesus Christ and his shed blood upon the cross, the barriers were removed. It is possible now for us to enter into a relationship with God through Jesus Christ.

Reconciliation is always at God's initiation. "And since, when we were his enemies, we were brought back to God by the death of his Son, what blessings he must have for us now that we are his friends, and he is living within us!" (Romans 5:10). Paul reminded us in several places that this reconciliation was at the initiation of God: "All these new things are from God who brought us back to himself through what Christ Jesus did. And God has given us the privilege of urging everyone to come into his favor and be reconciled to him. For God was in Christ, restoring the world to himself" (2 Corinthians 5:18, 19). "As parts of the same body, our anger against each other has disappeared, for both of us have been reconciled to God. And so the feud ended at last at the cross" (Ephesians 2:16).

It is at this point that we see the great difference between Christianity and all the world religions. In the world religions the picture is that of man seeking God, man reaching for God. But Christianity is God seeking man, God taking the initiative. Christianity is God moving in love, sacrificing himself in order to bring redemption and reconciliation. The peace of God comes to us by faith through the grace of God. This comes not because we deserve it but because we need it and because God loves and cares for us. That is the great distinction between Christianity and world religions. Christianity is what our God has done for us.

". . . You, that were sometime alienated and enemies in your mind by wicked works, yet now hath he reconciled" (1:21, KJV). Here we have a reminder of the past. The word "alienated" means "foreign," "strange." We were foreigners, strangers from God. We get our word "alien" from this Greek word. We did not belong to God's kingdom. We could not communicate and fellowship with God. At one time we were separated from God. Everyone is a foreigner and a stranger from God apart from the shed blood of Jesus Christ. His blood is the only way we become a part of the family of God.

Paul described their alienation: ". . . and enemies in your mind" (KJV). Our thought life was in rebellion against God. The greatest danger to every individual, even the Christian, is in the mind. Every act of rebellion that comes into our lives starts in our minds. It is true that sin is the result of lust and rebellion in our hearts, but the origin is in our minds.

Our minds never shut off, even when we are asleep.

Whatever we dwell on and whatever we feed our minds will set our lusts into action. The Apostle Paul described those who were enemies and foreigners from the kingdom of God as being "enemies in [their] mind." We had better give attention to what we put into our minds. Our minds do not need much encouragement to become reprobate. We need to be careful about what we see on television, what movies we watch, what books we read. It is imperative that we protect and guard our minds because every act of rebellion against God originates first in the mind, in our thoughts.

A man who is lost is lost by his own choice, because he has exercised his mind in rebellion against God. He has chosen to turn against God. He has not been put in a position of condemnation by an irrevocable decree of God. Many people who call themselves Christian are not saved at all because they are still enemies of God in their minds. If there is anything we love to put into our minds more than the truth of God, there is something desperately wrong about our relationship to God. It does not matter what it is. The enemy of the best is not the worst, but the good. We can put a lot of good things into our minds that keep us from the best things. Beware! Those who are enemies of God are enemies first in their minds.

The thought life continues to be a cause of concern for the children of God. We wonder why we no longer feel the presence of God moving in our lives the way we once did. Our thought life may be the key, which is one reason we ought to memorize Scripture. We need to focus our minds on the eternal truth of the Word of God, to memorize the promises, taking the Word with us, whether it be on memory cards or small testaments. We must let it become a part of our lives.

Paul wrote that we were " . . . alienated and enemies in [our] minds by wicked works" (1:21, KJV). What we think about, we do. If we think about something long enough, we will do it. If we think about immorality long enough, we will do it. If we think about embezzlement and dishonesty long enough, we will be dishonest. Think it and we will end up doing it. There are many times we dismiss thoughts as being harmless fantasies. There is nothing harmless about anything that is in our minds.

"Yet now he has brought you back as his friends" (1:21). By the grace of God our minds have been changed. We are no longer enemies in our minds, shackled by the thoughts and rebellious deeds of our lives. We are no longer strangers to the kingdom of God. By the grace of God, all of that has been changed. Now we are heirs of God and joint heirs with Christ. We have been bound together with him. The past was full of rebellion and wickedness, but by God's grace we have been reconciled and great changes have taken place.

A PRESENTATION

"In the body of his flesh through death, to present you holy and unblamable and unreprovable in his sight" (1:22, KJV). It is possible that Paul emphasized the "body of his flesh" because of the Gnostic heresy that was so prevalent in Colosse. Certainly such a reference was appropriate. One of the basic tenets of Gnosticism was that all matter was evil and everything spiritual was good. So, nothing good could ever be of matter, and nothing bad could ever be of spirit.

The Gnostics had a problem when it came to understanding the person and work of Jesus Christ. One branch of the sect, called the *Docetics*, declared that Jesus was not really human, but that he just appeared to be. They taught that when he walked in the sand, for instance, he didn't leave footprints. Some feel that this was the basis for the Apostle Paul's saying, "Yes, he did have a body and it was in that body that God wrought reconciliation."

Whatever the expression means, it is very clear that the Apostle Paul was saying that the human nature of Jesus Christ was a necessary instrument to reconciliation. It was through his death *in his body*—through the shedding of his blood—that we are redeemed.

The word "present" is the same word used in Romans: "I beseech you, therefore, brethren, by the mercies of God, that ye present your bodies a living sacrifice, holy, acceptable unto God" (Romans 12:1, KJV). It literally means "to make us fit to stand in the presence of a holy God." The purpose of reconciliation, or redemption, is to make us fit to stand before God. Paul wants us to stand before God "holy, unblamable, and unreprovable" (1:22). The word "holy" is a word with two distinct characteristics or meanings. It means "wholeness" or "completeness." It is a reminder to us that we are never a whole person until we are whole in God. It further means "separation to God and separation from evil."

The aim of reconciliation is holiness. A popular concept today suggests that because God loves us so much he will not condemn our sin. To put it more mundanely, once we are saved, we can live like the devil and it is all right. That is not so! The aim of reconciliation is holiness, and anyone who continues to live in rebellion against God gives no evidence of having been saved. The greatest obligation in the world is placed upon those who receive God's love. It is the obligation to be worthy of that love. And that is what he proposes to do. When he saves us, he plants his Spirit in us and that Spirit enables us to be what we could never be by ourselves.

"Unblamable" literally means "without blemish." It reminds us again of the Old Testament sacrifice in which the animal to be sacrificed had to be perfect. A blind, crippled, or deformed animal was not acceptable for sacrifice. When Jesus Christ reconciled us, he did it as the perfect, unblemished sacrifice so he could present us "without blemish" to God.

"Unreproachable" is really a continuation of the idea of "unblamable," but it means more than being free from blemish. It means being free from the charge of it. We carry no scars from it. That in itself can give us some concept of what forgiveness means. God won't see us as forgiven sinners when we stand before him in judgment. He will see us as if we had never sinned because the blood of his Son, Jesus Christ, has "cleansed us from all iniquity." As far as the east is from the west has God removed our transgressions from us. He has buried them in the depth of his forgetfulness. God declares that "their sins and iniquities will I remember no more" (Hebrews 10:17, KJV). It is a beautiful thought that we will stand unreproved before God, not as forgiven sinners with our sins in his remembrance. He won't see them at all. Cleansed! That is good news in a bad-news society. He wants to present us holy, unblamable, unreprovable in his sight.

The phrase "in his sight" is a compound word in the Greek, which means "to look down in." It speaks of a searching, penetrating gaze. God knows all and sees all. He sees in the hearts of those who have been reconciled only holiness, blamelessness, and unreproachfulness.

So total and complete is the reconciliation Jesus effected that we stand holy, unblamable, and unreproachable before his gaze. That is what reconciliation means. We ought to be careful how we treat such a reconciliation. It ought to be the serious pursuit of our lives.

A PRESERVATION

"If ye continue in the faith grounded and settled, and be not moved away from the hope of the gospel, which ye have heard, . . ." (1:23, KJV). There have been some who have said, "That means the only way he can present us holy, unblamable, and unreprovable is if we continue in the faith." That means that if we don't continue in the faith, we will lose our salvation and the opportunity to be presented to him. In the original language, the "if" is not subjunctive or conditional. It is not merely some future sense of expectation. It literally states that we have been saved and that we will be presented holy, unblamable, and unreprovable. This is demonstrated by our continuing in the faith. The word "if" in the King James Version is a translation of a word that often might be translated "since," as in this case.

We do not continue in the faith in order to retain our salvation, but as evidence that we do possess salvation. It is not the struggling after salvation but the possession of salvation that Paul was writing about here. If someone lacks the evidences of salvation in his life, it does not mean that he has lost his salvation; instead it is evidence that he never possessed it. One who has been saved will continue in the faith and be grounded and settled.

The word "grounded" speaks of a firm foundation. The word "settled" speaks of the stability of a building. While the verb "settled" is in the past tense, the word "grounded" is a perfect participle, which means that something happened in the past but it still has present benefits. That is what happened when we got saved. We received a once-for-all salvation, but it has permanent results in our lives. We were saved from the consequences of our sin, but that was only the beginning. That act stands established in the past and continues to produce evidence in our lives. We are grounded and settled in the faith.

"Continuing in the faith" is not a question of doctrine but of our commitment to Christ, our walk with the Lord, our hungering and thirsting "after righteousness," our deep desire to be in his will, and to please him. Because we have been saved, we are standing firm in our commitment to Jesus Christ.

"And be not moved away from the hope of the gospel" (1:23, KJV). The Gnostic heresy was a perversion, a religious fad. Because we have been grounded, rooted, and settled in our commitment to Christ, we will not be moved away. No matter what religious fads come along, there will be a stability of our position. We will not be moved away from the hope of the gospel. Some people chase every religious fad that comes along. God has provided a way to protect us from that—the Bible. What is truth? What does the Bible say it is? It is simple. Trusting God is not complicated, but a matter of believing him. We do not test truth by experience. We test truth by revelation, by the Word of God. We continue in the faith and we are not moved from the gospel because we are grounded in Christ.

Any theology, any religious thought, any experience has to be tested by the Word of God. How do we determine if something is right or not? By the Book! What does the Word of God say? We are rooted and grounded in the faith, so we stay with it. We measure life by his measuring stick. We measure truth by his revelation. We measure our conduct by his Word. Thus, we stand strong.

James said, "But when you ask him, be sure that you really expect him to tell you, for a doubtful mind will be as unsettled as a wave of the sea that is driven and tossed by the wind; and every decision you then make will be uncertain, as you turn first this way, and then that. If you don't ask with faith, don't expect the Lord to give you any solid answer" (James 1:6-8). Our continuing faithfulness to our commitment to Christ is evidence that we are fit to stand in the presence of a holy God. We will stand before him holy, unblamable, and unreprovable in the presence of his searching gaze.

"This is the wonderful news that came to each of you and is now spreading all over the world" (1:23). This gospel is universal in its scope. Every place we know, this gospel is destined to go.

"Whereof I Paul am made a minister" (KJV). The word "minister" is the word "servant." Doubtless, to Paul's mind, he was a servant to the gospel to which he was committed. It was his joy and privilege to declare the gospel. And that same joy and privilege is ours.

6

The Hope
of Glory
Colossians
1:24-29

"BUT PART OF MY WORK is to suffer for you; and I am glad, for
I am helping to finish up the remainder of Christ's sufferings for his body, the church. God has sent me to help his
church and to tell his secret plan to you Gentiles" (1:24, 25).
Notice the concept Paul had of himself as a servant and a
steward. Rejoicing in sufferings is not a normal response to
suffering.

To what suffering did Paul refer? Apparently his enemies
had come to Colosse and had begun to question the gospel
that Paul was preaching and to suggest that it evidently
could not take care of him since he was in jail. If God was
really what Paul said he was and if Paul had the truth as he
said he had, then God should be taking better care of him.
Paul's enemies could have made this suggestion which
could have been the stimulus behind Paul's statement. Or,
perhaps his accusers were saying to the people in Colosse
that if Paul really loved them, he would somehow come to
them and touch their lives. Whatever the background, it is
astonishing that Paul would state that he rejoiced in his
suffering.

What enabled Paul to rejoice in suffering? He could rejoice because he knew the reason and the nature of his

suffering. He saw it as part of God's purposes for his life; whatever God allowed to come was to better fulfill those purposes. He knew he was suffering in order that he could further the gospel. He saw it as the price tag he had to pay in order for the church to become more firmly established and to expand.

Paul told the Roman Christians that "all things work together for good to them . . . who are the called according to his purpose" (Romans 8:28, KJV). Later he talked about the fact that nothing could separate them "from the love of God which is in Christ Jesus. . . ." He mentioned all the things that could oppose, disillusion, or put pressure on them, saying that none of these things could separate them from the love of Christ. Paul saw in his sufferings the hand of a sovereign God. He believed with all of his heart that his sufferings were there for a purpose and that the church would ultimately benefit because of them. He did not necessarily understand it, but he believed that he was suffering in order to enhance the work of Christ. So he said, "I rejoice." What an amazing attitude! What would we be willing for God to do in our lives in order to have his purposes accomplished?

The Apostle Paul knew he was suffering unjustly at the hands of hostile enemies, who did not believe his Christ. When we put that attitude beside the selfishness that often attends our lives, we realize how far we have to go to be the servant, the steward God wants us to be.

" . . . For I am helping to finish up the remainder of Christ's sufferings for his body, the church" (1:24). That thought may pose some problems for us because it almost sounds as if he were saying that Jesus didn't suffer enough and that he, Paul, had to suffer in order to complete what Jesus had left undone. We know that is not true. Had he been saying that he was entering into the sufferings of Christ which were not yet fulfilled, then he would have called himself the redeemer or the mediator and not the minister or the servant. It is obvious he didn't have that in mind.

A better clue to understanding this verse is Paul's use of the word "afflictions" (KJV). This Greek word was never used in relation to Christ's suffering or redemption. Paul was saying that a hostile world opposed Jesus Christ, inflicted punishment, suffering, and persecution on him and that same hostile world will do the same thing to anyone who identifies with Jesus. ". . . They persecuted me," Jesus said, and "they will persecute you. And if they had listened to me, they would listen to you" (John 15:20). Paul was simply saying that the hostility that Jesus Christ faced and had predicted for his followers, had now touched him as Christ said it would, so Paul rejoiced in that kind of affliction. He saw it as being for the continuation, blessing, encouragement, strengthening and maturing of the Church.

"Whereof I am made a minister, according to the dispensation of God which is given to me for you, to fulfill the word of God" (1:25, KJV). The word "dispensation" is made up of two Greek words, one which means "house" and the other which means "law." It is translated in other places "steward." It refers to the law by which a household is governed, to the principles by which a family is managed.

Paul was carrying out the task assigned to him by God. It was God's ministry, God's task, God's church. God had given the law by which we are to live and God had made Paul a minister, a steward, within that relationship. It was a God-given stewardship and authority.

The false teachers at Colosse claimed to have authority. They claimed to be responsible. Paul said, "Unlike these false teachers, God gave me this responsibility and made me a servant over the household of God." This kind of servanthood speaks of service, responsibility, and authority.

The President of the United States is a servant of the

people, according to the Constitution. We elect him to direct the affairs of state. We have given him principles by which he is to govern. Our representatives in Congress have authority, but they also have responsibility. They have a framework in which to work, and are assigned a responsibility to serve the people through that framework.

Paul claimed to be a servant who had received his assignment, not from a constitution or a body of people, but from God himself. He had a stewardship of responsibility. Everyone of us has the task of the stewardship of our lives and the responsibilities to go with it. Each Christian is in the body of Christ, and as part of the body, we are linked together, having responsibilities that bear upon each other. Only as every person assumes his responsibilities as assigned by God within the body can the body function and progress as God intended.

Those who sit in the pew have been given their responsibilities just as the pastor in the pulpit has been given his. Each of us has been given an assignment. Paul was given the assignment to be a minister according to the dispensation of God which was given to fulfill the Word of God.

What did Paul mean by "fulfilling the Word of God"? First, his responsibility was to proclaim faithfully the Word of God. That is the task of the church, the assignment given to us. But it means more than that. The Word of God is not an ancient relic around which the church of God gathers to gaze. Rather, it is to be a living Word, applied to our lives. To fulfill the Word of God means that we preach and apply it so that it comes alive through its principles living in us.

The Word of God is not information for our heads. It is inspiration and energy by which we live for God. We should not say we believe the Bible if we do not live the Bible. Implicit in the gospel is a practical expression of obedience that needs to be incorporated into every life. Our

responsibility is to be obedient to the Word of God. We are
stewards of what we have received. We are under responsibility to assimilate into our lives every bit of biblical truth
which we have also incorporated into our minds. It is time
we quit talking about how much we believe the Bible and
begin to live by it.

MYSTERY

"He has kept this secret for centuries and generations past,
but now at last it has pleased him to tell it to those who love
him and live for him, and the riches and glory of his plan
are for you Gentiles too. And this is the secret: *that Christ
in your hearts is your only hope of glory*" (1:26, 27).

The Word of God contains a mystery. Certainly fulfilling
the Word of God means to expound, to explain, and to declare the mystery: God loves the Gentiles who have access
to him just as the Jews do. We preach that and proclaim it
so that the Gentiles can come into a saving relationship
with Jesus Christ. In times past it was not apparent what
the mystery meant, but now it is a "revealed secret" that
the Gentiles have equal access to God. That was a hard
lesson for the Jews to learn and accept. They had thought
for so long that they were the only ones God cared about,
and then they were told that the gospel included the
Gentiles.

From the very beginning, it was in the heart of God to
carry the message to the Gentiles. Some of the Jews understood that, but it was still unacceptable to many of them.
The spreading of the gospel to the Gentiles was not "Plan
B" that God put into effect when the Jews turned him
down. God had sent Jesus Christ, to be the Savior of not
simply the Jewish people, but of the entire world. That is
why John wrote, " . . . He is the propitiation for our sins:
and not for ours only, but also for the sins of the whole

world" (1 John 2:2, KJV). This mystery was now made apparent. God's eternal purpose for his people was that they know the wonders of his redemption and his love and the depths of his concern for all the world.

"To whom God would make known what is the riches of the glory of this mystery among the Gentiles" (1:27, KJV). It is difficult to explain these brilliant superlatives: " . . . the riches of the glory." The word "glory" speaks of the effulgence, the brightness of the purposes and presence of God. It is a word sometimes ascribed to God himself. Paul spoke about the "riches" of this brightness. The only way I know to express this is to say that God wanted to make known the blazing brightness of the truth of his love for all mankind.

The Gentiles were once shrouded in darkness but now they had the light because Jesus Christ had come for them. It seemed that God's concern had been narrow and included just the Jews, but Paul explained that God had determined to make known to all people "the riches of the glory of this mystery."

And here is the mystery: "Christ in your hearts is your only hope of glory" (1:27). That in a nutshell is what the gospel is all about—Christ in us. Paul explained it elsewhere: "That out of his glorious, unlimited resources he will give you the mighty inner strengthening of his Holy Spirit. And I pray that Christ will be more and more at home in your hearts, living within you as you trust in him. May your roots go down deep into the soil of God's marvelous love; and may you be able to feel and understand, as all God's children should, how long, how wide, how deep, and how high his love really is; and to experience this love for yourselves, though it is so great that you will never see the end of it or fully know or understand it. And so at last you will be filled up with God himself" (Ephesians 3:16-19).

To the Galatians, Paul wrote: "I have been crucified with Christ: and I myself no longer live, but Christ lives in me. And the real life I now have within this body is a result of my trusting in the Son of God, who loved me and gave himself for me" (Galatians 2:20).

Christ in us is the hope of glory. Christ in us is the expression of salvation. The world does not need to see an imitation of Christ—it needs to see Christ *in* us. We can never be like Jesus; however, Christ can be himself in us, which is what Christianity is all about. Having anything less than Christ in us should cause us to come in confession and repentance to God. In helplessness and openness we respond to his claims so that he can come into us.

That is the mystery that had been hidden for so long and now has been made manifest. It is still the greatest source of joy the Christian can know. If Christ is in us, his presence will drive away the tempter, along with those things that can alienate and divide us. Christ ruling and reigning in our lives is our hope; that is why it is so vital for us to commit ourselves to maintaining our daily relationship with him. The only way his power and presence can control our lives is for us to walk with him day by day. If we are going to walk with God, we must walk where God walks. As long as there is disobedience, rebellion, or refusal to follow his will for us, Christ cannot live through us in the way he longs to do. We do not make him live—we permit him to live in us.

Our willingness, our openness, and our acknowledgment of our needs are the key. The trouble with most of us is that we are too self-conscious. The Christian through whom Christ truly lives and in whom Christ reveals himself is one who lives daily in an awareness that he cannot do it without the Lord. We cannot walk one day without him nor face one trial without him. Being a Christian is not a matter of our handling the easy things and letting him handle the hard things. It is our letting him do it all. Only Christ can be in us the victory that we need. This is the mystery now revealed: Christ in us.

"Whom we preach . . ." (1:28). The word "preach" speaks of declaring something that is already heard. It speaks of something that has been accomplished and is a declaration of that fact. "We are preaching the accomplished fact of Jesus Christ." Notice Paul said, "Whom we preach," not "what we preach." It is not speaking so much of doctrinal preaching of what we believe but a declaration of something that has already taken place. It is not so much preaching informational truth but preaching the person of Jesus Christ.

"Warning every man, and teaching every man in all wisdom . . ." (1:28, KJV). Here are both the negative and positive aspects of the gospel witness. The word "warn" speaks of admonitions regarding sin, judgment, and the need for repentance—the negative aspect. The teaching is positive instruction in Christian truth. Preaching Christ includes both aspects. There are a negative aspect of a call to repentance and a positive aspect of declared truth.

Paul said we are to preach and teach "in all wisdom." That does not mean that what we say is necessarily brilliant or highly intelligent. It is not talking about content. It refers to the manner in which we preach Christ. In other words, we are not irrational fanatics. We do have an intelligent concern for this world, and we will convey it in an ethical and truthful way.

We read throughout the New Testament an admonition for us not to preach the truth, but also to preach it in the right way. Some people can preach the truth in an irrational, detrimental way; others can take the truth about the judgment of God and preach it as though God takes great delight in judging people. Anytime we preach on God's chastisement, on hell, or on the retribution of God against evil, we ought to do it with a broken heart because God does not delight in judging the sinner. Paul declared that we must preach, warn, and teach in a way that is believable, effective, honest, and ethical.

The purpose of this preaching is "that we may present every man perfect in Christ Jesus" (1:28, KJV). Paul was reflecting on the time when the Lord Jesus Christ will return and all earthly ministries will be finished and every believer will be judged by the Lord. The purpose of warning and of preaching is that we may all be presented perfect or mature, full grown, accountable, and responsible in Christ Jesus.

"Whereunto I also labor..." (1:29, KJV) speaks of wearisome toil. It reminds us that there are many obstacles in the Christian life, many enemies who fight and war against our maturity. If Satan cannot keep us from getting saved, he wants to keep us from growing in Christ. He will do everything he can to keep us babes in Christ, responding and reacting like baby Christians. He will do everything he can to keep us in spiritual kindergarten, to defeat us, and to make us miserable. When we give ourselves to Christ, we will have obstacles placed in the path of our Christian maturity. Facing obstacles is difficult and discouraging—it requires hard work.

"Striving according to his working..." (1:29, KJV). The word "striving" means "straining, stretching to the limit of endurance, reaching as far as we can." That sounds like work. There is no place in God's kingdom for a lazy person. We talk about resting in the Lord, but resting in the Lord doesn't mean being lazy or living for our own comfort. Paul was not talking about an easy life.

But notice that Paul was striving "according to God's working." From the word "working" we get our word "energy." This word is always used in reference to God's working, never man's working. It is always used of supernatural power, supernatural energy. Paul labored according to God's energy. God's working in us does not lessen our need to strenuously and actively serve him. Paul's labors and struggles would not be futile because God would empower him. God was working through him and blessing his efforts. His labor was not in vain because God was working through him by a power which surpasses human understanding. Paul would give himself in work, but when it was all said and done, it was God who had done it.

God expects us to be usable. To be usable, we have to be busy and active for him. That does not mean that we race a 100-yard dash all the time. There is a time for long slow races in training. There is a time for exercise, as well as for rest. It is not to say we have to be in a dead run all the time. We tend to feel that being busy means we are doing something, which is not necessarily true. God is going to work through active people to achieve his ends, through energetic people who have a vision and a dream of what God can do, through people who are willing for God to use them.

We can work and serve in the energy of the flesh, but God won't use that part of our efforts. We serve him, we labor, and we strive. But it is his working that works mightily in us.

That seems to be contradictory. We talk about God doing it and about our doing it. We talk about God working and about our working. The heart that longs to please God, that lives for God, that truly has Christ living and reigning in it is a heart located in an active body that is working, serving, and touching lives. May God reveal that mystery to us, clearly manifesting to us that we are to labor according to his working. Our part is to be willing, open, and obedient. When we are, his part is to assign us to the task and to work mightily in us through his power.

7
Full Knowledge of Christ
Colossians 2:1-7

"I WISH YOU COULD KNOW how much I have struggled in prayer for you and the church at Laodicea, and for my many other friends who have never known me personally" (2:1).

Many people live their lives without any great commitment to anything. Many spend an entire lifetime doing what is required of them and very little more. They live simply on the basis of getting by, with no real commitment or dedication to anything.

Other people live their lives with zeal, with deep devotion and deep commitment. They go the second mile, and in their hearts are a love for the Lord and a dedication to him. This passage speaks of just such a person.

The Apostle Paul was a man with the world in his heart. He said, when he wrote to the church at Rome, whom he had never seen, "I am a debtor to all men. I have a debt to you. I have something I must do for you." And he lived his life under that deep and abiding sense of urgency, mission, and commission.

CONFLICT

Paul spoke of conflict. The word "struggled" speaks of intense strain. It is the Greek word *agonea*, which was used earlier (1:29), from which we get our English word "agony." Translated elsewhere as "striving," it speaks of intense effort, as of an athlete preparing for competition. The athlete gives everything he has, strains, and uses all that he has learned in training. To use the word in connection with prayer shows the tremendous burden and struggle going on in Paul's heart on their behalf.

For what was he struggling? Not from outward enemies against his comforts or his culture. His great conflict was because of his great concern over dangerous doctrines being taught in the churches at Colosse and Laodicea. Doubtless, he understood that he had a great responsibility to those people. He called them "those who have never known me personally." Yet he felt concern and a responsibility for them. He understood that this struggle was not for himself.

He was burdened for them because the gospel was still new. He felt that if his word were discredited, if the false teachers succeeded in tearing down what he had proclaimed and the people believed the heretical doctrine that was being taught by the Gnostic teachers, it would destroy the work he had done for God.

Our most intense struggles are usually not for ourselves. The honor of Christ and the faith of others are in our keeping. We stand with the name of Christ, and it is his honor that is ascribed to our character and to our teaching. The faith of those whom we know and affect is in our keeping. Gnosticism is not dead. Today we are seeing a great rise of what I would call twentieth-century Gnosticism. It is the cult of the intellect, which believes that accepting the old conservative viewpoint is a mark of ignorance.

I wrote to an editor of a Sunday school magazine about a certain issue. He wrote me back and said that he had been exposed to a cross section of biblical scholarship that I had not seen, which is exactly what the Gnostics said. They believed they had learned something no one else knew, that they had a teaching that satisfied and appealed to their minds which was the way to God.

The attacks of Satan and those who oppose the teaching of the Word of God have never changed. These claims of intellectual superiority which we are hearing are not new. We must not get so comfortable that we are not able to grieve and agonize over that which is significant to the cause of Christ.

COMFORT

"This is what I have asked of God for you: that you will be encouraged and knit together by strong ties of love, and that you will have the rich experience of knowing Christ with real certainty and clear understanding. *For God's secret plan, now at last made known, is Christ himself*" (2:2).

When Paul used the word "hearts," he meant the totality of the personality—the mind, the emotions, and the will. The word "encouraged" does not mean that they were sad and needed to be cheered as if they were grieving. He agonized, prayed, and gave his life in order that their faith might be confirmed and courageous as they stood for the Word of God.

He prayed that they would be "knit together by strong ties of love." Heresy always divides, splits up, and destroys unity. Paul agonized in prayer so that they would be knit together in love, for without love for God and for each other, there is no real church. When love dies, the church dies. One of the great things we need today is an explosion of love where God's people love and care for each other. This could truly bring a revival. The pattern of the church today is one of devisiveness and separation rather than one of love and concern for each other.

Paul prayed "that you will have the rich experience of knowing Christ with real certainty and clear understanding." As long as we are uncertain about what we believe, we will be vulnerable to any idea that comes along. Spiritual prosperity consists of understanding God's truth and being confident in it. Too many people today are spiritually poverty-stricken because they are uncertain of what God has provided for them. They become easy victims of every cult and every religious charlatan that comes along.

"In him lie hidden all the mighty, untapped treasures of wisdom and knowledge" (2:3). What is the treasure? It is Christ. But, it is not Christ in his incarnation, in his life, or in his death or resurrection. It is not Christ in his ascension or his return. Those are not hidden at all, but had been plainly spoken about prior to this time. The mystery hidden before is the union of the believer with Christ, being one with Christ. Being joined with him is the hidden mystery. We have been joined to him by his Spirit. We possess his life. One with him, we are being destined to share his glory. That is the wonderful mystery that was hidden and is now revealed. How little we all know of the treasure that is ours in Christ! If we could only comprehend what Christ has provided for us, it would take us an eternity to know and enjoy all its treasures. Unsearchable riches!

CHRIST

The truth in Christ is not a secret hidden, but a secret revealed. It is not something to be concealed, but to be openly preached. The Gnostics said that their great volumes of truth made up their deep understanding of the way man finds God. Paul declared that Jesus Christ is the revelation of all truth. He called it "untapped treasures of wisdom and knowledge," using two words to describe what happens when we fully comprehend our relationship with Christ:

"wisdom" and "knowledge." "Knowledge" means "the ability to grasp a truth, to understand it intellectually." "Wisdom" means "the ability to apply the truth to life." One speaks of information and the other speaks of inspiration.

In Christ we do not have just knowledge for the head though there is enough knowledge in Christ to cause the mind to spin into an eternity of intellectual hunger and pursuit. It is more than a truth for the mind to conceive; it is for the life to live. That is why the New Testament repeats the reference to "doing the truth." Truth is not just for information for the mind, but is inspiration for the way we live.

Christ is all we need. He is everything we need to know. To that end, Paul agonized, struggled, and gave his life even for those he had never seen, which helps us understand the commission of the church a little bit better. We are to give the great pursuit of our lives, not only to build the body that we can see, but to touch lives in every corner of the earth, people we have never seen. We do that so they may be encouraged, established in the faith, and enter into the full understanding of all that it means to be joined together with Jesus Christ.

WALKING IN CHRIST

"I am saying this because I am afraid that someone may fool you with smooth talk. For though I am far away from you my heart is with you, happy because you are getting along so well, happy because of your strong faith in Christ. And now just as you trusted Christ to save you, trust him, too, for each day's problems; live in vital union with him" (2:4, 5).

Paul continued to warn of false teachers who would distort the truth. It apparently was not uncommon for religious charlatans to parade through the early church. The New Testament often contains many warnings to the church about testing the doctrine and trying the spirits to determine if they were of God or of Satan. Apparently many went about making their living off Christian people, just as it happens a lot today. Some people simply go from church to church across the country telling their story, which may or may not be entirely based on truth, and draw a living off God's people.

It has always been that way. However, back in Paul's time, some were trying to destroy the soundness of the faith. The church did not have the New Testament Scriptures that we have. Consequently they depended on the apostles' teaching of the truth. There was much concern in the early church that the truth be accurately taught and received, a concern which Paul reveals in this passage.

THE CHURCH'S DISCRETION

Notice first the church's responsibility. "And this I say, lest any man should beguile you with enticing words" (2:4, KJV). An intriguing combination of words is used here. The word "beguile" means "to deceive, to reason falsely, to cheat by false reckoning, by telling something and concluding something that is not accurate." The word was used in the courtroom to describe the words of a legal counsel who would disguise the truth in his appeal to the jury and judge. Many times a guilty man might go free because of the persuasive talk of the one who defended him. The word "beguile" speaks of those who would use their rhetoric, ability, and talent to speak words of deception. They used enticing, attractive, appealing words, sounding as if they knew what they were talking about.

The church is supposed to use discretion in those matters. Just because someone sounds as if he knows what he is talking about does not mean that he does. In our day we have great evidence of this very thing. No one sounds more knowledgeable than some of the cult leaders who appear on television and radio. Some of them are masterful in the use of words. When one turns the dial on the radio and hears them, he automatically stops and listens. But that does not mean that the speakers are telling the truth or preaching the gospel.

Just because someone is eloquent is no reason to assume he is truthful. The church must exercise discretion and see the very fine line between truth and falsehood. In fact, the most dangerous falsehood is that which is the closest to the truth, not some heresy that denies everything good, godly, and wholesome, but the heresy that sounds the most like the truth. That heresy is the most difficult to discern. The more eloquent a man may be, the more determined, convincing, and persuasive in his speech he may be, the more difficult it is to determine whether or not he is telling the truth.

So much that sounds true today is not truth. A man recently said, "I believe that the Bible is the inspired Word of God and that God's perfect revelation was Jesus Christ." Sounds like the truth, doesn't it? But when I inquired further, I saw that he did not mean what we mean by "inspired." In truth, he denied the only record we have that Jesus came. His original statement sounded good, but it was not good. The child of God needs great discretion today. We are bombarded from every side—radio, television, magazines, tracts, and pamphlets. What is truth? The Bible declares that the church needs to be able to discern it. Because Jesus Christ is wise and holds all knowledge, he will guard us lest we be beguiled with enticing words.

We are living in crucial days as far as heresy is concerned. In fact, this is perhaps the most crucial time the world has ever known. We stand on the verge of national collapse and face the possibility of global holocaust. Many signs point to the destruction of our society as we know it. If there were ever a time when a "Thus saith the Lord" needs to be sounded, it is today. Never has there been such an attack upon truth. Our greatest enemies are often in the Christian community. Great discretion is needed as we listen to those who would beguile us with enticing words.

The early church had a simple formula. If the Word of God did not substantiate what they were taught, they discounted it. There is a good pattern for us. We just need to look at the Word. It is one thing for a man to have a different interpretation. We will not argue over interpretation. But when a man denies the Scripture, then we have nothing to interpret. We need to be very careful that we stand upon the Word of God, which is our authority. If the Word of God is not the foundation, then we ourselves are. There are only two choices—either a divine authority or human authority. There is no other choice. Either we accept the Word of God or we accept the word of man.

THE CHURCH'S DISCIPLINE

When Paul spoke of discipline, he was not just talking about the discipline of the membership, taking action against a sinning brother. Discipline has to do with the kind of life we live, the commitment we have, our spiritual discipline that expresses itself in our personal devotion, and with our personal consecration to Jesus Christ.

" . . . Though I am far away from you my heart is with you," Paul wrote (2:5). We have a fellowship in Christ's body that distance cannot sever. His prayer and concern for those people brought him into their presence through a fellowship and spiritual bond that distance could not diminish. What a tremendous thing God has given us as we share together in the fellowship of the church!

Paul was rejoicing in what he saw of the Colossian Christians. Though he was not with them in the flesh, he was with them in spirit, rejoicing as he beheld their united fellowship and strong faith. If we could understand the meaning of the word "getting along," it could revolutionize our churches. The Greek word is *taxin*, a military term translated "order" in the King James Version. It speaks of the cohesiveness or unity of the military unit. In the context of the church, it speaks of a unity of faith and a unity of conduct which bound these Christians together like an army. In a military unit, every man has a job. The secret of success for the army is for every man to be in his place doing his job, standing in his position, doing what he is commanded to do. The church is a great army of Christians. Every man stands in his appointed place, ready and willing to obey the command of his Lord. No wonder Paul was rejoicing in the obedience, commitment, and discipline of these Christians!

Remember the story of Gideon and his men as they fought the vast army of Midian. Only 300 people were used of God to destroy the enemy. At the climax of the story, the Scripture declared, "And they stood every man in his place round about the camp" (Judges 7:21, KJV).

Imagine what would occur if in the church all of the people understood their assignments and accepted their appointed positions. We could shake hell itself with a group of people like that! Paul rejoiced because they were a disciplined church, a church of order, where people accepted responsibility, were faithful to their assignments, and were willing to respond to the Lord's commands.

No wonder we have such a hard time today. We have built an army which only the generals are responsible to fight. We do not have the concept of everyone having a responsibility, a place of service. I wish that all who joined our churches would come knowing that God had a place for them to fill and they would come reporting for duty. Today, if we want something done, we hire someone to do it. The Apostle Paul said that it was his purpose to equip the saints for the work of ministry. He did not say that his job was to minister, but to equip the saints to minister. Leaders in the church, often by default, have taken over assignments that do not belong to them. It may have been done out of ego or something else, but God never intended it that way. God put the church together like a body, and every member of that body has an assignment. Paul said, "I praise God for your order. Every one of you is in your place, you have accepted your assignments, and you are doing your job."

He further spoke of their "strong faith in Christ." We do not change subjects here because the word "strong" is also a military term. It speaks of an army that is set in an immovable formation. The assault of the enemy can come, but that formation is unbreakable, unbendable. Think of the church, hand in hand, arm in arm, standing together, and the assault of hell beating upon it. But it stands, unbreakable, unbendable, and immovable.

"And now just as you trusted Christ to save you, trust him, too, for each day's problems; live in vital union with him. Let your roots grow down into him and draw up nourishment from him. See that you go on growing in the Lord, and become strong and vigorous in the truth you were taught. Let your lives overflow with joy and thanksgiving for all he has done" (2:6, 7).

Paul described their conduct as being "in vital union with him." Jesus Christ was the object and source of their faith. Jesus is the Alpha and the Omega, the beginning and the end. He is the heart, the circumference, the substance, object, and source. In him we live and move and have our being, as Paul said.

"Trust" is a common word meaning "listening to and receiving the instruction of a teacher." It is in the "aorist" tense, which speaks of past, completed action, an action that has been consummated in the past but continues to have present implications. At a point in the past we trusted Christ, but the fact that we trusted Jesus continues to determine how we live now.

Our lives are lived on the basis of our reception of Jesus, of our commitment to him. We trusted him in the past but we continue to live for him. Paul was emphasizing over and over again that our lives need to match what we say we believe. We prove by our lives the validity of the gospel we claim to believe.

The aorist tense emphasizes the decisive nature of that reception. It also carries with it an emphasis of the continuity of the transmission of the gospel. The Colossians received the gospel by word of mouth, the manner in which the gospel is to be spread. We receive it and we give it. The word and the tense used tell us that it is important that we continue the transmission of the gospel we have received. That is the purpose of the church.

The word "walk" (KJV) refers to the normal pattern of living. Walking is the normal way of getting around. It refers to our lives. Literally it says, "Continue to walk in him." It speaks of steady progress. We share his life as he lives in us. Our conduct, our deportment, is evidence that we belong to him.

The beloved physician Luke said of Peter and John that the people "took knowledge of them, that they had been with Jesus" (Acts 4:13, KJV). They could not hide it. The fact that they had been with Jesus stood out. They had walked in him and they could not keep back the fact that they belonged to Christ.

Paul described this walk. "Let your roots grow down into him and draw up nourishment from him. See that you go on growing in the Lord, and become strong and vigorous in the truth you were taught. Let your lives overflow with joy and thanksgiving for all he has done" (2:7). The perfect participle "grow down" speaks again of actions in the past. Like a plant, we are rooted in him; just as the roots are the life of a tree, so Christ is the source of life and strength for us as we draw from his resources. When we were saved, we were rooted in him (perfect participle). There is no question that something happened in the past that continues to be meaningful now.

The next verb, "draw up," is in the present passive tense. It literally says, "having nourishment drawn up from him." The King James Version translates it "built up," using the symbolism of a building. We ought to walk like a man, be rooted like a tree, and built like a building. Paul was not bound to any singleness of thought but used many figures of speech to describe our relationship to God. Being built like a building is the picture of Christ as the foundation which holds the building together, a reminder of the fact that the Christian life is not something that happens once and for all but is a continuation. Just as a building is built layer by layer upon the foundation, so the Christian life grows and matures as it is built in him.

The Christian life is not a swift accomplishment but a life-long process. The tragedy is that so many people have ceased to grow in the process. What a tragedy that they have no memories of today but only of "back there."

The word "stablished" (KJV) means "to become increasingly stable and firm in the faith, in what we believe, in what we stand for, in how we live."

The phrase "you were taught" reminds us that we have a responsibility to teach the Word. People must be taught before they can be held responsible for what is being taught. It is a beautiful witness to the assignment given to the Church. That which we have received is ours to commit to faithful men who will in turn teach others (2 Timothy 2:2).

THE CHURCH'S DISPOSITION

Paul wrote "Let your lives overflow with joy and thanksgiving for all he has done" (2:7). The apostle had a feeling that if the people really understood what Jesus had done for them, they would be glad and grateful. It is difficult for us to understand that.

We have never seen anyone crucified, nor probably seen anyone attacked by a mob, severely beaten beyond recognition. We have probably never seen someone put through the mockery of a trial where mob rule and injustice prevailed. We don't have any accurate concept of what Jesus has done for us. The disposition of the church is to be one of gratitude and thanksgiving.

When I think of what Christ has done for me, every day becomes a time of praise and thanksgiving. I thank God every day that he doesn't give me the justice I deserve. If we could live in an increasing awareness of his mercy, how grateful our hearts would be! How sad that we are so selfish, always prone to complain about what we don't have, and so seldom really thankful for what Christ has done for us.

8

Complete
in Christ
Colossians
2:8–15

"DON'T LET OTHERS SPOIL YOUR FAITH and joy with their philosophies, their wrong and shallow answers built on men's thoughts and ideas, instead of on what Christ has said" (2:8).

It is possible for one to warn someone of a danger in such a rude manner that the warning itself is offensive. The Apostle Paul could have done that, but he was also very careful to compliment and to encourage the people at Colosse. He expressed his happiness when he saw their order and steadfastness of faith. Then he gave a gentle warning absolutely necessary for all ages, including ours.

FALSENESS

He began by saying, "Don't let others spoil your faith and joy" (2:8). In the present imperative, it meant "keep looking" or "be constantly on the look" or "never relax your vigil." We should never become careless in our Christian lives. Careless people get hurt. One of the great dangers of working on a manufacturing assembly line, of doing the same thing over and over again, is that workers become so familiar with what they are doing that they become careless. Losing their sense of concentration, they consequently may do something harmful.

The Christian life is that way. One of the dangers is to become so familiar with Christian truths and with the ritual of worship that we take them for granted and become careless. We don't seriously, diligently stand watch in our faith as we should.

Paul was warning against such carelessness. "You think you will never believe the wrong thing or be swept away by the wrong teaching, but beware!" The word "spoil" means "to capture so as to make a slave." It speaks of a free person being captured and bound, which is exactly what heresy does.

The false teachers who came into the church at Colosse were the ones Paul was warning the church about. He was concerned that they would become bound by their false teaching. He said, "You have been set free and delivered from falsehood by the power of Jesus Christ. Don't be in bondage again."

The word "philosophies" comes from a combination of two Greek words that mean "the love of wisdom." There is nothing wrong in loving wisdom. We are admonished throughout the Word of God to be wise. Jesus is called the "Wisdom of God." The King James Version speaks of "vain deceit." "Vain" means "futile, empty, without purpose." We must not let someone lead us astray with a philosophy that has no meaning, no foundation. Paul was concerned that these Christians might let some eloquent teacher come into their midst and tell them something intellectually fascinating, but empty, vain, and destructive to their faith.

Paul described the philosophies as being "built on man's thoughts and ideas." The easy way to tell heresy is to ask, "What did God say about it?" Whatever teaching we want to know about can be easily discerned by putting it beside God's Word. If God didn't say it, then man said it. We must not be led astray and enslaved by humanistic philosophy built after the tradition of men. Just because man passed it down doesn't make it acceptable since tradition can be either good or bad.

The phrase "rudiments of the world" (KJV) probably relates to astrological terms. In the ancient world, astrology was a dominant concern. It would be difficult for us to describe the emphasis that the stars and astrology played at that time. These Gnostics, who claimed a superior knowledge, had told the Colossians that wisdom was found in the stars. "Rudiment" means "elemental factors." It could mean "things in a row." It referred to the alphabet and could mean the elemental truth of anything relating to the world of astrology, or the order of the spirit world these Gnostic teachers had thought up.

The truth is still there for us today. Anything not built on Jesus Christ has to be rejected, no matter what it is. The horoscope, the zodiac, and astrology are of the devil. One shouldn't confuse astrology and astronomy. Astronomy is a reputable science, while astrology is a humanistic philosophy built on man's fantasy. The zodiac signs are not even consistent with science in terms of the location of the stars and the other heavenly bodies, which are supposed to exert an influence on us. The falsehood about their influence was a problem then just as it is today. Any Christian who gives any thought or any leaning to astrological predictions and astrological calendars is playing a dangerous game.

FULLNESS

" . . . In him dwelleth all the fulness of the Godhead bodily" (2:9, KJV). In the original language, "in him" is stated as an emphatic. It means "in Jesus and nowhere else dwells the fullness of the Godhead." The word "dwell" means "permanent residence." The fullness of God dwells in Jesus. It always has and always will.

It would be difficult to give a more accurate translation of "fullness." It means completeness. These false teachers said that Jesus was one of the rays of light of God's glory and if we really wanted to know God's glory, it would come through the secret of their philosophy. Paul's rebuttal was "Jesus is no mere ray of light. He is everything, the fullness, the completeness of the Godhead bodily."

"Human body" refers to his incarnation and to his glorified body. It is in the continuous tense, which means he continues to be even now the fullness of God himself. Paul was referring to Jesus' pilgrimage here on earth and now his glorified state in heaven. In Jesus Christ alone dwells permanently all the completeness of the essence of God, actually and physically. We are complete in him.

The word "complete" (KJV) is the same root Greek word translated elsewhere "fulness" (KJV). Our fullness is based on his fullness. We have God because we have Jesus. The "rudiments of the world" refers to these mystical philosophies of the stars and spirits. Paul, however, said that "Jesus is the head of all principality and power." They thought they had full knowledge, but without Jesus they had nothing. Jesus is the head of it all, the one who put the stars in their places. He is the governor, the king of all principalities and powers.

Even if some philosophy sounds Christian, we don't need anything other than Jesus. We cannot get any fuller than full! We talk about being filled with the Holy Spirit, but we are really talking about giving Jesus full liberty in us. In Jesus dwells all the fullness, and we are full in him.

FORGIVENESS

"When you came to Christ he set you free from your evil desires, not by a bodily operation of circumcision but by a spiritual operation, the baptism of your souls. For in baptism you see how your old, evil nature died with him and was buried with him; and then you came up out of death with him in a new life because you trusted the Word of the mighty God who raised Christ from the dead" (2:11, 12).

Circumcision was a physical cutting away of the flesh from the body. It was an external act, done for ceremonial, as well as practical, purposes—for cleanliness. Even the Old Testament fathers did not believe or interpret the act of circumcision as being purely physical, for the Old Testament talks about "the circumcision of the lips," "the circumcision of the heart," and "the circumcision of the spirit." They understood circumcision not only as a physical act of obedience to God, but also as something that was reflected in a change of life.

These false teachers told the Colossians that they needed to be circumcised physically in order to be saved. Paul, in this passage, told them it was a work of God in their lives to deal with the sinful nature. Salvation was not just a cutting away of a portion of the flesh, but a putting away of the power of the flesh.

"Putting off" (KJV) is a combination word. One of the words means "getting out of your garment." It is prefixed by a preposition, and gives the meaning of "getting out of your garments and getting away from them." It means not only taking them off, but also abandoning them.

We have been forgiven and our forgiveness is not simply a cutting away of a portion of our flesh. Rather it is a cleansing, forgiving, and liberating from the power of our flesh. God's forgiveness did not eradicate the sinful nature, but it took the power away from it. We no longer have to be controlled by the power of the flesh, living for physical appetites to please the flesh. We have been freed from that. We have a cleansing, a forgiveness, a circumcision from God of the spirit and the heart. What Jesus does in our hearts can only be accomplished by him. It is not the promptness, the punctuality, or the meticulousness to the ritual and ceremony of religion that cleanses, but the redemptive work of Jesus in our hearts.

If our hearts haven't been changed, we haven't been saved. If there is not a different attitude toward ourselves, acknowledging our sinfulness, weakness, and helplessness before God, then nothing has happened. If there has not been a change in our attitude toward others where there is a deep love and compassion and concern; if we have not felt a yearning of our hearts to share the Word of God and to enhance the kingdom of God in this world, then nothing has happened in our hearts.

Forgiveness is internal. But it expresses itself externally. Most commentators believe that the phrase "buried with him" refers to water baptism, which is the outward sign of the inner change, just as circumcision was an outward sign of the inward change. Baptism is the external evidence that we have given our hearts to Christ. In Paul's day, when a man was baptized, he was coming out of heathenism into Christianity, not just from the Methodist church to a Baptist church or from a sect of the Christian church or from the Roman Catholic Church. He was coming out of heathenism.

Baptism represented dramatically and vividly what had happened in one's life. Baptism refers to death, but also to resurrection. It shows the end of an old way of life and the beginning of a new life. And it represented a resurrection to a new life. Many times a man who was baptized would lose his family, or his property would be confiscated. He himself would sometimes become hunted as an outlaw among his own people. It might have cost him everything. His baptism was a symbol that he had burned his bridges behind him, that he was not going back to his past. He had given his life to Christ and died with the One who had died for him. Jesus had given him new life, and he was raised to walk in that new life. It was not a symbol taken lightly.

We are saved neither by circumcision nor by baptism, but

by faith in Christ. Faith is the channel or the means by which we receive the forgiveness of God. The key is faith, "because you trusted the Word of the mighty God" (2:12).

DEADNESS

"You were dead in sins, and your sinful desires were not yet cut away. Then he gave you a share in the very life of Christ, for he forgave all your sins, and blotted out the charges proved against you, the list of his commandments which you had not obeyed" (2:13, 14).

Prior to coming to Jesus Christ, the Colossians were spiritually dead. The difference between a lost man and a saved man is the difference between death and life. Over and over again this comparison is made. Jesus said, "Indeed the time is coming . . . when all the dead in their graves shall hear the voice of God's Son and shall rise again" (John 5:28). He wasn't talking about the cemeteries coming to life. It is obvious he was talking about those who are spiritually dead, those with physical life but with no spiritual vitality. The person who is lost in sin is described as being spiritually dead with no more power over his life to overcome sin or to atone for it than a dead man has. No man in his own strength can resurrect himself.

This deadness in sin manifests itself in several ways. Some sins are a violation of the standards of God, which is what the word "sins" means. It is like running a red light. The law says, "Stop," but we go through, violating the standard. A person who is dead in sin has a life-style that is in violation of the standards and principles of God. One of the ways we know we are saved is that there is in our hearts a desire for a life-style in accord with the purposes of God. A person who claims to be saved but has no desire to be obedient to God's standard gives no evidence of being saved.

This deadness is manifested not only in deeds and in life-style contrary to the standards of God, but also in a fleshly nature that is hostile to God. "Your sinful desires were not yet cut away" (2:13). A person dead in sins lives on a sensual level, on the basis of human nature with its lust, greed, and selfishness. He violates the standards of God. Living purely on a physical, material level, he is devoid of the life of God and is motivated by a totally depraved nature.

We are sinners by nature and by practice. We are by nature dead. By practice we live in the uncircumcision of the flesh. A person who is not saved is a sinner by nature and by practice.

Knowing this, we can more easily understand passages such as: "Whosoever abideth in him sinneth not" (1 John 3:6, KJV). On the surface, it appears that if a person ever commits a sin, he is not saved. But the consistent witness of the New Testament and indeed of that passage conveys the idea of habitual practice. A person who is born of God does not habitually live according to the dictates of the flesh and the world. If he does, he is not saved.

DELIVER

The passage also speaks of deliverance. Paul used several phrases to describe it by showing what happens when one gives his life to Jesus Christ in faith. People say, "I am doing the best I can." They are having a hard time if they are. If you want frustration, then just do the best you can. God's deliverance is manifested in special extraordinary ways.

"Then he gave you a share in the very life of Christ" (2:13). We have been raised in him. Paul said we are buried with Christ in baptism and risen by faith in the operation of God (2:12). Paul continued this description of deliverance as having passed from death unto life. Jesus said that we no longer belong to the realm of darkness but have come to the light. A person delivered from sin has been brought to life in Jesus Christ.

"For he forgave all your sins" (2:13). From the word "forgave" we get our word "grace," a beautiful description of forgiveness, which is God's mercy giving to us what we could never deserve. But he gives it to us anyway. Forgiveness is grace. We are not forgiven because we do certain things in the power of the flesh. Even the faith we have is a gift of God.

Our repentance is also a gift, something God has allowed us to do in response to his Spirit. When we are forgiven, we can never say, "I did what God told me to do so I am forgiven" because forgiveness is an act of God's mercy. Our tendency to think of ourselves and others as "supersaints" must grieve God.

The Word of God declares that our deliverance through Jesus Christ comes at the prompting and the moving of his grace. Forgiveness is something we desperately need and do not deserve, never something that we have a right to expect or demand on the basis of anything we do.

Paul said that God "blotted out the charges proved against [us]" (2:14). When we borrow money, we sign a contract. Our names on the contract acknowledges the debt. In ancient times, such a transaction would be handwritten. The handwriting of charges described a writer's confession of debt.

The reference to "commandments" in this passage doubtless refers to the commands or laws of God, as though Paul were saying to them, "You did not measure up to the law of God, so there is a list of grievances brought against you in writing to which you signed your name, confessing your guilt."

God's deliverance of us removed the confession of debt and marked it "Paid in Full." Blotting out of the charges, however, is something else. In ancient times, two types of writing material were used. The papyrus was similar to our paper, but vellum was made of certain kinds of animal skin. The ink contained no acid. When it was used to write, it did not bite into the paper or the animal skin, but just adhered to the surface. It would dry and could be read, but it was not indelible. Sometimes a scribe might need some extra writing space and all he would need to do was to take a sponge and wipe off a space. The ink, not having bitten into the surface of the vellum, would release itself and come clean. Then the scribe would use it for writing again.

When Jesus Christ died on the cross, and we accepted him as our personal Savior, we were delivered so completely that God, through the shed blood of Jesus Christ, took that handwritten statement of guilt and wiped the surface clean. It is not just paid in full although that is true, but it is gone, removed, blotted out, without a trace. God banished the record so completely that nothing of it remains.

How many times have we said to ourselves, "I wish I could start all over again." We can! God not only forgives, but also forgets! We can face every day free from our guilt. Our part is to acknowledge our sins to him. His Spirit draws us, moves in us, calls us. When we respond to him, we are delivered so completely that he not only pays our debt in full but also wipes it off the record as though it had never existed.

Paul spoke of "charges proved against [us]." This means we are on the debit side of the ledger—in the hole, no assets. When he spoke of the things "which you had not obeyed," a stronger phrase is used that most translations don't indicate. The handwriting against us put us in debt. The ledger we have signed acknowledges that we are in debt beyond our ability to pay. But the word "contrary" (KJV) carries it a step further, speaking of hostility toward us because of our debt. It is like having our bills turned over to a bill collector who hounds us and stays after us, threatening and intimidating us. Until we are delivered from our sins, we are on the debit side of the ledger. The sins that we have charged against us haunt us and we are never free from them. That is why we need to be delivered through Jesus Christ. He removes it from the ledger: ''he destroyed it. . . .'' Forgiveness is complete. First, we are made alive; then we are forgiven. Then the sins are blotted out, and finally he destroys the ledger, ''nailing it to Christ's cross,'' (2:14).

Jesus was resurrected from the dead, but our sins weren't. When Jesus died on the cross, our sins died with him—our debts died with him. But when he was raised, he left them behind. That means forgiveness is complete.

How can a child of God still live under the despair, depression, and dominion of his sin? Can he not see what Jesus has done to his sins?

The whole picture is one of being accused, or more accurately, blackmailed. It is as if someone has our signed confession and is blackmailing us. The book of Revelation calls Satan the ''accuser of the brethren.'' He accuses us not only before God, but also to ourselves, always reminding us what we used to do, what we used to be. Satan is always reminding us of our failures. He even reminds us of our successes if he can get us to have the wrong attitude about them. But he is always accusing us of sin, disobedience, and rebellion in order to destroy us. But he doesn't have anything against us if God has taken our signed confession and blotted it out, erasing it completely.

God wants us to live on the basis of total cleansing, total forgiveness. When we enter into a relationship with God through Jesus Christ, he wants to give us forgiveness. If we still feel guilty, we are not dwelling upon the promises of God that tell us we are forgiven.

''And having spoiled principalities and powers, he made a show of them openly, triumphing over them in it'' (2:15,

KJV). Some think Paul was referring to the power of Satan, but others think he was referring to the powers of good angels. It makes no difference. All principalities and powers are subject to Jesus, who is the head of all principality and power. There was a time when God mediated his message by revealing himself through angels and messengers, through powers higher than man. When Jesus came, that mediation passed out of existence. When the veil of the temple was torn, it was ripped from top to bottom as if God's finger had split it. There is no longer any separation. Jesus has perfectly atoned for the sins of men. Jesus brought perfect meaning and fulfillment to the message of the Old Testament.

Whatever "spoil" means and whatever "principalities and powers" means, they simply point out that Jesus took control of a situation that was bound to destroy man and spoiled the principalities and powers. Jesus triumphed "over them in it" (2:15). He is the only message of hope to men in frustration and despair. Jesus Christ crucified and risen is Lord of all. Redemption in Jesus Christ is a cosmic redemption—of all mankind, of all principalities and powers.

The whole creation groans in pain until the redemption that will come in Jesus Christ (Romans 8:21, 22, KJV). He who is Lord of all the universe is also Lord in our hearts.

The God of the telescope is also the God of the microscope. Just as we look into a telescope to see outer space, we can look into a microscope and see the vastness of inner space. The God of all is the God of our hearts.

The sovereign God of creation is also our God, our Savior. He loves us, knows when we hurt, and is never too busy to listen, never too occupied to respond to our need. He demonstrates his greatest power when he reduces himself to transform and change our life as in the new birth he gave to us, when he made a public display of his power, cancelled our debts, and gave us victory through his life.

9

A Shadow
of Things
to Come
Colossians
2:16–23

"SO DON'T LET ANYONE CRITICIZE YOU for what you eat or drink, or for not celebrating Jewish holidays and feasts or new moon ceremonies or Sabbaths. For these were only temporary rules that ended when Christ came. They were only shadows of the real thing—of Christ himself" (2:16, 17).

After having told the Colossians of their freedom from sin, Paul now warned them of becoming bound up again. They once were bound up in ordinances and bound by their sin, but they had been set free by Christ.

RITUAL

The word "criticize" (2:16) means "to take to task, to put under condemnation, to enslave." "Let no one take you to task or judge you guilty," Paul admonished.

Some say that Paul was referring to certain forbidden foods. Some foods were clean and acceptable to eat, and others were unclean and forbidden. It is possible that he was talking about foods, but more than likely, he was referring to something else. The arrangement in the original language of "what you eat or drink" refers to the act of eating and the act of drinking. Part of the Gnostic heresy was that everything physical was evil. Because of these ascetic ideas, it seems more correct to conclude that Paul was saying, "Don't let anyone judge you on the basis of whether or not you eat or whether or not you abstain from eating," which was part of the legalism within the Colossian church. He may also have referred to some of the Jewish ordinances that forbade certain kinds of foods. At any rate, he warned them not to let someone enslave them again or take them under the bond of legalism or ritualism.

Legalism, in whatever form it takes, is man's way of saying that God needs man's help in our salvation. Paul was saying, "Don't let anyone tell you that you have to be bound by certain nonbiblical ordinances of man in order to know God."

He also included ritual and ceremony: "Celebrating Jewish holidays and feasts or new moon ceremonies or Sabbaths" (2:16). Some of the religious festivals involved quite a lot of pomp and ceremony. The new moon, for instance, in which messengers were sent to the highest mountain peaks to signal the first rays of the moon was quite a production. They heralded the new moon with trumpets and fanfare and all sorts of ceremony.

"Don't let anyone judge you," Paul said, "with regard to ritual." It is not wrong to use ritual, for ritual refers simply to a pattern of doing things. Ritual may awaken our emotions, stimulate our thoughts, strengthen our faith. Ritual may provide precious vehicles of the truth. But ritual may become meaningless if we substitute it for the Lord Jesus Christ. Then it is not only meaningless, but also dangerous and injurious.

Paul explained that rituals "were only shadows of the real thing—of Christ himself" (2:17). The picture is very clear. Some have thought the word "shadow" refers to an outline, but it means a shadow like the ones cast by our bodies when we walk in the sunlight. If we did not have bodies, we would not cast shadows. A shadow is the result of the body, even as ritual is the shadow of a certain other body—the reality which is Christ.

Paul was drawing a picture of all the ordinances and rituals of the Jewish system as being mere shadows, of which the substance was Christ. The function of ritual is practical and not ascetic. It is not something necessarily beautiful to see, but something to look through. The important thing is not the way we observe the ritual, but what the ritual helps us to observe. Even if rituals are good, and ordinances meaningful—and most of them are—they are just shadows of the substance of our worship.

REWARD

"Don't let anyone declare you lost when you refuse to worship angels, as they say you must. They have seen a vision, they say, and know you should. These proud men (though they claim to be so humble) have a very clever imagination" (2:18, 19).

The words "declare you lost" are very closely related to the word translated "criticize" in verse 16. These words, however, mean "to decide against or to declare unworthy of a prize." Paul was saying, "Don't let anyone say you do not get the prize. Do not let anyone rob you of your reward." These Gnostic teachers, claiming a superior revelation, told the Colossians, "You don't have the glory of Christ that you think you have. You do not have those rewards." But Paul told them, "Do not let anyone declare you unworthy of your reward."

Then Paul described how the false teachers would try to beguile them with a false or imitation humility. In our day, we would say it is someone who is proud of his humility. When we become conscious of our humility, it ceases to be a virtue. It ceases to be a blessing and becomes a point of pride.

How subtle Satan is! If he can't keep us from being humble, he will let us know how humble we are and make us proud of it. That is what these false teachers were doing, declaring that the Colossian Christians were unworthy of the reward that was theirs in Christ by a self-conscious humility. It was really a conceit, an arrogance, a pride, yet they called it "humility."

We all know people today who are very proud of their so-called humility. We have found new words like "brokenness." If we have really been broken, we don't have to tell anyone. We talk about "Lordship." If Jesus is really our Lord, we don't have to tell anybody. When we do, it becomes a point of self-conscious pride.

We really haven't come too far from the Pharisees, who thought the way to impress people with their piety was to pray on the street corner where they could be seen in all four directions. They would have trumpets declare when they were about to give offerings. They made a big production out of religion. Jesus warned that if we do what we do to be seen of men, the pleasure we get from being seen is our only reward. Paul said they came in, telling them how spiritual and humble they were, but actually sought to rob men and declare them unworthy of their rewards.

The mention of angels is a reference back to the external form of worship. If an angel is worshiped, then the angel becomes the intermediary between the individual and God. A system of worship or a form of external worship that includes angels takes us back again to being slaves to ritual.

Paul said the false teacher was " . . . intruding into those things which he hath not seen" (2:18, KJV). The word "intruding" speaks of a diligent search. In the best manuscripts the word "not" does not appear. The reason is that this is a "tongue in cheek" remark, probably sarcastic, meaning "they seek to rob you of your reward by searching diligently into their alleged vision." They "claimed" special insight and "special" revelation from God. The wording is very obvious. Despite their claim, these false teachers were searching into the things they really hadn't seen. It could have been hallucinations or self-deception, but most likely simply fraudulent claims.

Paul said the false teacher was " . . . vainly puffed up by his fleshly mind" (2:18, KJV). "Vainly" means "futilely, worthlessly." "Puffed up" means "arrogant, proud." Of their so-called revelations Paul said, "Not anything of the kind. It is just the old flesh, the old sinful mind. There is no higher reason. It is just man's fleshly mind." Paul again was cutting away at the basis of the false teachings.

The logical conclusion, which is tragic, is explained: " . . . They are not connected to Christ" (2:19). They had become so attached to ritual and traditions that they were not attached to Christ. That is inevitably the result when one affixes himself with devotion to ritual without affixing himself with devotion to Christ. When ritual and ordinances become one's passion, life is inevitably insecure, uneasy, and dissatisfying. Inevitably one runs into a dead-end street and life is frustrating and depressing. The only way the body can have life is to be attached to the head. One who holds onto ritual and ceremonies is not holding onto the head.

Believers "are joined together by his strong sinews and we grow only as we get our nourishment and strength from God" (2:19). The "strong sinews" nourish and hold us together, and there is strength available for the whole body to function. The body, being nourished and knit together, increases with the knowledge of God. The false teachers, in their false humility, their slavery to ritual, did not have hold of Christ. But the body, attached to the head, receives nourishment and grows. Notice it is the nourishment from God and his strength that profits. There is not one aspect of human nature, not one thing about our character, that is pleasing or acceptable to God. Nothing we can do in our human strength will help us be what God wants us to be. From the head and into the body comes an increase from God.

There is to be something supernatural about our lives. We are to walk in his power, grace, strength, and life—that can only be as the head gives nourishment and strength to the body. Only here is the finite truly united with the infinite. Everything the symbols and rituals of the sacrificial system were established to declare, we have in Jesus.

The hope of our lives is not for us to learn to act like Jesus or to stop before we do something to ask, "What would Jesus do?" We are to be so joined with him that growth, strength, and life from God will flow naturally. It is not our doing things for him, but his doing things for himself through us. It is not our determination to be true, to be faithful, but our willingness to be obedient. The increase that comes is the increase of God.

However good ritual and ordinances may be biblically, we will still be judged by Christ. We must not let anyone rob us of our reward. We must not let anyone make us feel that they have a greater revelation or higher spirituality than we have.

The very fact that someone would declare such a revelation disqualifies him and reveals that it is just a product of his fleshly mind. It is through Christ that strength and nourishment are ministered. Through him we are knit to the Body of Christ, and our only hope is his moving in us and living in us.

SUBJECTION TO ORDINANCES

"Since you died, as it were, with Christ and this has set you free from following the world's ideas of how to be saved— by doing good and obeying various rules—why do you keep right on following them anyway, still bound by such rules as not eating, tasting, or even touching certain foods?" (2:20, 21).

The rules about eating or drinking reflect asceticism. Some said that certain foods were evil and had to be avoided. Rather than simply categorizing foods and drinks, they required that at certain times of the year, one would completely abstain from certain ones. Though Paul mentions only food in this passage, doubtless there were many other taboos in this religious community. Paul was trying to enlighten the Colossian Christians of the subtle heresies involved.

Asceticism is the belief that depriving the body of certain normal desires helps achieve a more complete holiness and approval of God. The Colossians were being told that by doing these things, God's approval could be gained and holiness could be achieved. This passage is a reminder that the things we do and don't do are not ends in themselves. We don't restrain from doing certain things in order to become holy, but because we are holy. We can't deprive our body of needed physical desires and drives and become more holy or more spiritual. We may not do certain things as children of God, but these things are the result of our relationship with the Lord.

When I really became serious in my relationship with God, there were some things that left my life. My vocabulary became limited. My activities were limited. But these were not removed from my life in order to make me more holy, but they were things that God crowded out of my life. I stopped doing certain things because his presence could not tolerate them.

There has always been a tendency to look at people's lives for a certain kind of conduct by which to judge whether or not they are spiritual. And bragging about spirituality becomes a contradiction in itself.

THE CONTRADICTION

Three things in this passage deal with this contradiction. "Since you died, as it were, with Christ and this has set you free from following the world's ideas of how to be saved—by doing good and obeying various rules—why do you keep on following them anyway?" (2:20). Paul was not casting doubt. He was basing his arguments upon the fact that the rules had been dead with Christ. Christ's death was the satisfaction of God's broken laws. There is nothing left for us to do to please God. There is a contradiction if we say we have died with Christ but are still subject to ordinances and believe that we must do certain things to be holy.

The phrase "world's ideas" ("rudiments," KJV), means "the world system," a system that is hostile to God and in opposition to him. Paul said, "You have died to that system. Why are you still living by the principles of an evil world?"

The world says, "If you hit me, I will hit you." Jesus said, "Turn the other cheek." The world says, "If you criticize me, I'll criticize you." Jesus said, "Don't return evil for evil." The world says, "You are to love your friends and hate your enemies." Jesus says, "You are to love your enemies." The Christian is to be distinct, unique, not a person ordered by the same goals and driven by the same principles as the man of the world. Paul pointed out the contradiction: "Why are you still subject to worldly standards when you have died with Christ?"

Death freed the slave from his obligation. If a slave died, he was no longer a slave, but free. The people in the New Testament world would understand that. They lived in an age of slavery and thus knew that a dead slave was no longer in bondage. Paul said, "Since you have died with Christ, why are you still living like a slave to the world?" A person still driven by sin and defeated by it has something seriously wrong with him, for if he is dead with Christ, he is not dominated by sin.

THE COMMANDMENTS

"Touch not, taste not, handle not..." (KJV) were prohibitions, being foisted on the Colossians. The verb "touch" here really means "to handle," "to cling to," "to fasten to." The word "handle" is a more casual type of touching, a more superficial contact. We could translate it roughly, "Don't handle this, don't taste that, don't even touch the other thing." There are many things that a Christian cannot do, not simply in order to become more spiritual, but because Jesus is in our hearts. We are free from that kind of legalism.

THE CONFUSION

Paul gave some very good reasons why we should not be subject to ordinances and not be bound by human regulations: "Which all are to perish with the using" (2:22, KJV). Everything we are told not to do is going to decay and disappear anyway. Why be bound by something that is transitory? Jesus spoke of this same truth: "Do ye not perceive, that whatsoever thing from without entereth into the man, it cannot defile him; because it entereth not into his heart, but into the belly..." (Mark 7:18, 19, KJV). Jesus was not saying we couldn't put anything in our mouths that would hurt us, but rather that we are defiled before anything ever goes into our mouths. It is not what we put in that defiles us; it is the sin that is already there.

Paul described the ordinances as "mere human teachings," not as God's restrictions or commands from the Bible. These were doctrines of men, inventions of the human mind.

In the time of Jesus, the legal system of the Old Testament had been recorded by the inspired men of old, but the Scribes and Pharisees had added a great host of oral traditions that were far more burdensome than any of God's commands had ever been. This is apparently what Paul was talking about—commandments and doctrines of men. We have to stand upon the Word of God because if we don't, then all we have will be the commandments and doctrines of men.

We can find the commandments and doctrines of men anywhere, but we find the doctrines of God in the Bible and no place else.

"These rules may seem good . . ." (2:23). The false teachers had created a legalistic system of how certain things were to be used. Such a system can become a burdensome assignment, a disguise for hypocrisy, and a superficial way of showing false spirituality. It looks good and appears to be spiritual. But Paul warned that these rules "require strong devotion and are humiliating and hard on the body." Such devotion refers to worship according to man's own will. To have such worship and humility together sets up a false criterion for spirituality leading to false pride, dissension among the brethren, a loss of direction, and a compromising of convictions. It leads to setting up standards based on the commandments of men.

Paul said such worship was "hard on the body," which simply means that it was depriving the body. Many of these ordinances related to food, drink, or sleep. His conclusion was very important: "they have no effect when it comes to conquering a person's evil thoughts and desires." All the ascetic prohibitions, the false guidelines, were of no value to them. The old flesh was still there, still craving for attention. It may have driven the lusts underground, but they were still there.

Nothing could be worse than for us to fast and spend our whole time dreaming about food. Fasting is of no value in conquering the gratification of the flesh. Fasting that is spiritual replaces our physical appetite with a fierce, insatiable hunger for God that leaves no room for physical appetite. Fasting may be beneficial when we are studying the Word of God, giving ourselves to prayer, or communicating with God. It becomes a spiritual exercise, not simply a physical abstinence.

The seat of our sinful nature is not our bodies, but our hearts. Jesus said, "Your souls aren't harmed by what you eat, but by what you think and say!" (Mark 7:15). Later he said, "It is the thought-life that pollutes. For from within, out of men's hearts, come evil thoughts of lust, theft, murder, adultery, wanting what belongs to others, wickedness, deceit, lewdness, envy, slander, pride, and all other folly. All these vile things come from within; they are what pollute you and make you unfit for God" (Mark 7:20-23).

Adultery is not just an immoral act of the flesh. An immoral act of the flesh is the result of evil rebellion against God in the heart. When we have attained some semblance of control of the body, if it has been purely on a legalistic basis and out of a sense of guilt or pressure, we will still not have satisfied the flesh.

I am not saying that a Christian should not live an exemplary, holy, good habit-filled life. Certainly we should. But we do it because within us is a nature that makes any other kind of action unthinkable. When we submit to the evil flesh that is within us and we sin, we are immediately confronted with it by the Holy Spirit. If we commit it to God, then we are cleansed from it. Man-made regulations do not satisfy. Only his presence, his purpose, his will, and his power in us can suffice.

10
Risen with Christ
Colossians 3:1-4

"SINCE YOU BECAME ALIVE AGAIN, so to speak, when Christ arose from the dead, now set your sights on the rich treasures and joys of heaven where he sits beside God in the place of honor and power" (3:1).

This passage immediately sets before us a distinction that needs always to be foremost in our minds—the fact that a Christian is to be a different kind of person from a non-Christian.

RISEN WITH CHRIST

"The Christian is risen with Christ," Paul said, "and the Christian will be revealed with Christ." The great apostle was continuing the symbol of baptism in which we are pictured as having been buried and then resurrected with Christ. Baptism speaks of a negative, something in the past, a death to the old way of life.

Resurrection speaks positively of the present and the future, pointing to a new kind of life. "Since you became alive . . ." is a positive affirmation of our resurrected life. It is best translated "in view of the fact. . . ." There is no doubt at all. Paul was speaking to saved people, who have had an experience of grace—people who have repented of their sins and have responded to Christ.

"Now set your sights on the rich treasures and joys of heaven, . . ." he said, describing how different a child of God ought to be. The words "set your sights" are in the present continuous tense, meaning "keep on setting your sights." It speaks of practical striving and devotion of our energies to heavenly things.

Paul was not talking about things "above" as if they were things in the future. Neither was he trying to get us to have "another world" attitude as if we can't do anything in this world. He says that we are not to live just for some future time, for he immediately gives specific things we can do in the present time. We are not to be so preoccupied with the future that we do not allow God to use us right now.

When Paul challenged the Colossians to keep on seeking the things which are above, he was reminding them that the Christian marches to the beat of a different drummer. We are no longer going to live our lives based on the standards of this world. We are going to set our "affections above where Christ sits on the right hand of God." We are not going to view the opportunities of this life from a natural perspective, but from God's perspective.

The secret of the early church was that they drove the world to God, to Christ. They were so committed and so different, so set apart from the pagan world, and their standards were so unusual in their godless society that they influenced the world for God. That is what we are supposed to do. In business, in pleasure, at home, at church, and wherever we are, we are to listen to God's instructions and set our lives by his standards.

The place where Jesus "sits beside God" is a place of majesty, a place of power and intercession. It is a place of holiness. We are reminded elsewhere by Paul, "Yet it was because of this that God raised him up to the heights of heaven and gave him a name which is above every other name, that at the name of Jesus every knee shall bow in heaven and on earth and under the earth" (Philippians 2:9, 10). Paul also described Jesus as "the one who went back up, that he might fill all things everywhere with himself, from the very lowest to the very highest" (Ephesians 4:10). Jesus Christ has supreme sovereignty; he pervades the universe. He is the one by whom and for whom the world was created. By him all things continue to maintain their structure and meaning.

Seeking things that are eternal, those things that are of Christ, requires our activity and energy. A faith that is anchored in Jesus Christ is going to be strong and practical. The faith that brings us to God changes our lives and thrusts us into the field of service with our energies directed for him.

"Let heaven fill your thoughts; don't spend your time worrying about things down here" (3:2). The idea is that we can direct our minds and thoughts. Paul kept coming back to the importance of what we feed our minds, what we think about. To set our affections, to direct our minds, to give our attention to things "above," is the proper mental attitude.

We often think about something a long time before we do it. What we think about then determines what actions follow, so we need to be very sure that we, who have been raised with Christ, set our thoughts on things "above."

Certainly there are many things worthy of our attention upon this earth, but that which pulls us away from our concentration on Jesus must be abandoned. Jesus said, "Anyone who wants to be my follower must love me far more than he does his own father, mother, wife, children, brothers, or sisters—yes, more than his own life—otherwise he cannot be my disciple" (Luke 14:26). Did he mean that we have to hate them, otherwise we don't really love him? Not at all. But if there ever comes a time when love for our family interferes with our love for him, there is no question as to which must go.

The same principle applies in this passage in Colossians. Some things are not worthy of our attention, and Paul listed some of them, as things we need to abandon. Though there are many worldly pursuits in which we must be involved, all of them are to be viewed in the context of setting our minds on Christ.

Any husband who loves his wife and loves Jesus as he should will be a better husband. Any wife who loves her husband and responds to him out of loving Christ will be a better wife. Any employee who does his job, knowing that he does it daily as "unto the Lord," will be a better worker.

We must set our minds on things "above," not on things on the earth. We must not give this world our first concentration, but must always seek the things of God.

So much of our service and devotion to God is almost an afterthought. We start eating and then remember we ought to thank God for our food. We go to bed and remember we haven't prayed. We should set our minds, direct our energy, to the things of God, in order to be better citizens of this world and approved citizens of heaven.

Setting affections and seeking those things above mean that we not only seek heaven, but also think heaven. A total involvement of our being, energy, heart, and body is required in serving him.

REVEALED WITH CHRIST
"You should have as little desire for this world as a dead person does. Your real life is in heaven with Christ and God. And when Christ who is our real life comes back again, you will shine with him and share in all his glories" (3:3, 4).

Paul explained why our thoughts should be about heaven and not earth. "For ye are dead, and your life is hid with Christ in God" (3:3, KJV). "Ye are dead" is in the past tense. "You have died" probably would be a better translation.

When we trusted Jesus Christ, we died with him, and our lives are now "with Christ and God." These beautiful phrases mean that the center of our energy is in Christ and not in the world. We find our source in him. He is our life, strength, foundation, motivation, reward, incentive. We are secure in Christ, hidden from the world. The world will never understand the Christian or why we attend church frequently or why we give our money and our time. They do not comprehend it because our lives are hidden from them. Because they are not spiritually discerning (1 Corinthians 2:14), we are a mystery to them and a cause for amazement and wonder. It also creates some hostility and consternation because they cannot understand that our lives are hid with Christ in God.

Notice that our lives are hid " . . . with Christ in God" (KJV). They are safe twice. Jesus said, "My sheep hear my voice, and I know them, and they follow me: And I give unto them eternal life; and they shall never perish, neither shall any man pluck them out of my hand. My Father, which gave them me is greater than all; and no man is able to pluck them out of my Father's hand" (John 10:27–29, KJV).

We are in Christ's hand and we are in the Father's hand. We are doubly safe, as we see also in this passage in Colossians. Our life is hid with Christ in God—with Christ because we died with him and were raised with him, and in God because that is where Jesus finds his life.

"And when Christ who is our real life comes back again, you will shine with him and share in all his glories" (3:4). Jesus is not just an influence on our lives. He is our life. He doesn't just move us to do good; he is good in us. He is the essence of life. There is no need for something new. If we want to be approved by God and to have the power for godly living, the answer is Jesus Christ.

Paul was obviously referring to Christ's second coming to earth. "When he comes back," Paul said—not "If he should come back." The day of his glory is future, but its arrival is as sure as if it had already happened, as certain as the events of past history. His coming is yet future, but we live in the reality of the victory right now.

Then, "you will shine with him and share in all his glories." When he is revealed, we will be revealed. We will no longer be misunderstood and despised by the world. When he shall appear, we shall appear; the world will see us, know us, and understand us.

The glory of God is veiled now. But when Jesus appears, the veil will be drawn back and the glory will be revealed. He, who came in humility and was despised and rejected among men, shall appear again in his glory, majesty, authority, and power. And we shall appear with him.

We don't understand all of what that means, but John said, "Yes, dear friends, we are already God's children, right now, and we can't even imagine what it is going to be like later on. But we do know this, that when he comes we will be like him, as a result of seeing him as he really is" (1 John 3:2). Having been raised with Christ makes a difference—a dynamic, practical, personal difference in our lives. We can live that risen life with him so that when he appears, we shall appear with him.

11

Challenge
to Purity
Colossians
3:5–11

"AWAY THEN with sinful, earthly things; deaden the evil desires lurking within you; have nothing to do with sexual sin, impurity, lust and shameful desires; don't worship the good things of life, for that is idolatry. God's terrible anger is upon those who do such things" (3:5, 6).

Christianity is far more than a creed or a doctrine. It is not confined to hymns, prayers, or programs, for it involves the continual response of the believer to the new life that is within.

We live on two levels. Spiritually, we are living in the age to come—eternity. Temporally, or physically, we are living and bound by this present age. Within us reside two natures. The old nature is not eradicated at conversion so that we are never again tempted. One reason a person makes a profession of faith and then later doubts his salvation is that he falsely assumes that getting saved meant he was no longer subject to sinning. In the New Testament we see that at salvation there are two levels of life within: the spiritual nature and the carnal, fleshly nature.

After Paul declared the beautiful truth that we have been raised with Christ to walk in newness of life, he continued: "mortify your members" (KJV). How do we reconcile that? If we are dead, why do we have to mortify our members? If we are risen with Christ, why do we have to go back and put to death our members again? Because we live on two planes. As a result, there is a continual struggle within us.

The New Testament over and over again speaks of the tremendous discipline and diligence that ought to characterize the Christian life. We can never assume that we have "arrived." Paul, after thirty years as a preacher-teacher-missionary-evangelist, said, "I am still not all I should be . . ." (Philippians 3:13). The child of God is to continually hunger and thirst after God. Jesus said, "Blessed are they which do hunger and thirst after righteousness: for they shall be filled" (Matthew 5:6, KJV). That struggle goes on all of our lives.

DEATH

Three words stand out in this passage. The first word is "death," which means "mortify." In our time that word has come to mean "a restriction placed on the body." If I mortify the flesh, I go on a diet or deny myself some desired physical pleasure. But that is not what the original word implies. In Greek the word literally means "to put to death." That is a drastic step. Paul was talking about putting to death our physical bodies, our arms, legs, eyes.

The New Testament, without apology, calls upon us to eliminate everything in our lives which is against God. Jesus said, "And if your hand—even your right hand—causes you to sin, cut if off and throw it away" (Matthew 5:30). We must go to whatever extent is necessary to eliminate whatever is against God.

The reason is very clear. This body will either be an instrument for God to use with the new nature that we have, or it will be an instrument for Satan to do evil with our old nature. The members of the body will either be avenues of temptation or the temple of the Holy Spirit.

Paul admonished the Colossians not to give the flesh free reign. Sin and rebellion come naturally. We do not have to teach a child to say no. It is unnatural for us to respond to God. It is God who draws the responses from us. We are to be sure that our members, our bodies, are not used as instruments of sin.

Paul told the believers not to yield their members "as instruments of unrighteousness unto sin," but "unto God" (Romans 6:13, KJV). That is a choice believers must make. Paul pointed out in this passage in Colossians the things believers can do to hinder their relationship to God. First, he mentioned "fornication" (KJV), a word in Greek from which we get our English word "pornography." It speaks of illicit sexual intercourse. When the New Testament was written, sexual immorality outside of marriage was common practice, an accepted thing. There was little, if any, awareness of purity or thought of restraint in the pagan world. To such a world the gospel was preached. Paul underscored that the child of God is a new creation and cannot look upon life and lust in the same spirit as one who is not saved.

Second, Paul mentioned "uncleanness" (KJV), which refers to the impurity of lustful living and sexual perversion. The extent of the perversion of that day is explained in Romans 1:28. Paul said that kind of living must be put to death.

Third, Paul mentioned "inordinate affection" (KJV), which speaks of lust, wicked cravings, and evil desires. It is in the heart that these things are born and where such acts begin.

"Evil concupiscence" (KJV) refers to sexual perversion and immorality, the kind we see in the Church today. Among the members of the Church there exist the same kinds of lust. People are becoming more and more careless about purity. If many who attended church on Sunday were exposed for what they are—immoral and adulterous—it would be the most embarrassing scene in the world.

We must face it. Our whole society is built upon the perversion of lust and sexual attraction. We are today in a period of license and have abused that which the Word of God clearly and repeatedly rebukes. The Word of God clearly says, "Put it to death."

Paul made an interesting conclusion by saying, "covetousness" (KJV). It doesn't really seem to fit the context. He listed all of the things relative to sexual impurity and then added "covetousness." The word literally means "a great desire to have more," which could have referred to desire for sexual, as well as material, things with which we generally associate covetousness. It is the opposite of the Spirit of Christ and real love, which longs to give. Lust wants to take, and covetousness means that we have within us the spirit to take, to pull to ourselves—not the spirit to give and to love, but to receive and to lust.

Covetousness is the most dangerous of all the sins listed because it seems to be the most respectable of all. But translate covetousness into any kind of desire in our hearts and it is the root of all kinds of sin. For instance, if we covet something someone else has, it could lead us to thievery. If we covet someone, it could lead to immorality. If we covet revenge or retaliation, it could lead to murder. If we covet, then the spirit of envy—jealousy, or greed—is in our hearts. But Paul said, "Put to death your members which are of the earth."

We must not let physical appetites drive us. We must not become so obsessed by the appetites of the flesh that we covet more and more.

DISOBEDIENCE

The second word that stands out in this passage is "disobedience." "God's terrible anger is upon those who do such things" (3:6). God is not an idle spectator, standing by watching with no real interest in what is happening. The word "cometh" (KJV) is in the present tense, speaking of present action. It tells us that God intervenes in our lives. He doesn't wait for us to die to pass judgment upon our lives, for the wrath of God is seen now. Sometimes the way God judges is to let sin take its natural course. He allows us to wallow in the filth of our own lust. To put it another way, he judges us by giving us what we want. Then we discover what a terrible thing we have asked when the consequences of our sin come upon us.

Three times we read, "God gave them up" or "God gave them over" (Romans 1:24, 26, 28, KJV). Paul told the Romans that God left them alone as a form of judgment. We don't want to be left with the consequences of sin and the evil nature within us. The wrath of God comes because of the disobedience of God's children, because we haven't mortified our flesh.

"You used to do them when your life was still part of this world" (3:7). He was not saying that they had necessarily committed each of the sins listed, but that they were characteristic of their life-style, their attitude of heart. Before they were saved, they lived in rebellion against God with no thought of the things of God. They lived in fornication and uncleanness. Even if they had never committed all of the sins, the desire and passion for them still controlled their lives. "But if you live that way now," Paul said, "you are disobedient." Over and over again, there is the emphasis in the New Testament that our salvation ought to show up in the way we live.

DISCARD

The next word that stands out in this passage is the word "discard," or "cast off." An old coat, for instance, that someone has outgrown is taken off and discarded when no longer useful. The word means to "strip off something that used to be a part of oneself and to do away with it."

If we have been raised with Christ, we must have a different attitude toward sin. Salvation means we have become new creatures. Old things are passed away, torn off, pushed to the side, discarded.

Paul said that believers ought to put off anger, referring to an abiding, habitual attitude of hostility. The word used is *orge*, which speaks of a sudden, violent temper, another sin that should not be characteristic of believers. People say, "Well, I just have a temper." They should let God have that temper, and stop justifying sin.

The word "hatred" means "a desire to injure or hurt someone." "Cursing" means "slander, or speech that is injurious to someone's good name." Christians sometimes do that in the name of prayer. They request prayer for someone and then tell all the garbage about the person, garbage that shouldn't be discussed. .

We sometimes slander in the name of Christian concern. The tragedy of slander is that the only thing a man can carry out of this world is his good name, and slander can destroy it. Paul said, "Put it off!" The desire to injure others has no place in the life of a Christian.

"Dirty language" speaks of foul, obscene speech—gutter talk. It doesn't take any intelligence to speak that way. It is significant that "cursing" and "dirty language" come after the mention of anger and hatred. When someone gives vent to anger and hatred, bad language often expresses it. The more perverted someone gets, the more likely he will curse or use foul language. The implication is that we either put off anger and hatred or else follow them with slander and obscene speech. Usually we are careless with the things we say when we are angry and distressed. Paul said, "Discard it."

"Don't tell lies to each other; it was your old life with all its wickedness that did that sort of thing; now it is dead and gone" (3:9). "Don't tell lies" is in the present imperative tense, a construction in the original language that forbids the continuation of an action already going on. Apparently these Christians had brought into the church the practice of lying to one another, which was common in the pagan world. The Christian's speech ought rather to be kind, not blasphemous or slanderous. It ought to be pure, not filthy or obscene. It ought to be truthful, not deceptive. Perhaps the greatest sins are those we commit with our mouths, for our words reveal what we really are. They can reveal wrath, anger, malice, lust, perversion, uncleanness, fornication, and greed.

We ought to have a different attitude toward sin because we are risen with Christ. Since we are controlled by a different master, we must discard the things that hurt and hinder and begin to show kindness in our speech, actions, and conduct.

PUTTING ON THE NEW MAN

"You are living a brand new kind of life that is continually learning more and more of what is right, and trying constantly to be more and more like Christ who created this new life within you" (3:10).

The previous passage spoke about the use of our physical bodies. Apparently lying or deception was one of the habits that these Christians had brought from their former lifestyle. Paul was saying their lives had to show a new lifestyle.

SALVATION

Paul reminded the Colossians of their salvation: " . . . seeing that ye have put off the old man . . . and have put on the new man" (3:8, 10, KJV). Being saved involves two aspects of commitment: the putting off of the old man with the old deeds and the putting on of the new man. From the structure of this phrase in the original language, the passage could read, "... having put off the old man..." or "the fact that you have already put off the old man means that now your life-style has to coincide with your experience. You have been saved, now you are to live like one who has been saved. You cannot continue with the deeds of the flesh, with those things that are characteristic of the old life-style." This is a common theme of the Apostle Paul as seen when he wrote to the Ephesians, "Then throw off your old evil nature—the old you that was a partner in your evil ways—rotten through and through, full of lust and sham" (Ephesians 4:22).

"Putting on the new man" is another common theme of Paul. To the Ephesians he also wrote, "Yes, you must be a new and different person, holy and good. Clothe yourself with this new nature" (Ephesians 4:24). To the Corinthians he wrote, "That is why we never give up. Though our bodies are dying, our inner strength in the Lord is growing every day" (2 Corinthians 4:16).

It is not enough that we just stop doing certain things. When we cease a way of life, we begin another. Our principles and our goals change. "When someone becomes a Christian he becomes a brand new person inside. He is not the same any more. A new life has begun!" (2 Corinthians 5:17).

SANCTIFICATION

These verses also give us a picture of sanctification, the process by which we grow into spiritual maturity. Our growth in the faith climaxes when we go to be with the Lord, or when he returns. The process begins at conversion and consummates in full redemption of the body and spirit.

Sanctification suggests continual renewal. Paul said, "But we Christians have no veil over our faces; we can be mirrors that brightly reflect the glory of the Lord. And as the Spirit of the Lord works within us, we become more and more like him" (2 Corinthians 3:18).

Paul seemed to make a play on words here. The Gnostics, those who were opposed to the true teaching of God, claimed to have superior knowledge and a better revelation. The word "knowledge" in this passage is the Greek word *epignosis*, which means "full, complete, perfect knowledge." So, with the claim of the Gnostics in mind, Paul was telling these Christians that they were renewed in perfect knowledge. Putting off the old man and putting on the new man brought his perfect knowledge into their lives.

The new man is "... after the image of him that created him" (3:10, KJV). Man was created in the image of God. Paul speaks about man being recreated in the image of God. The Spirit of God works the miracle of creation in our hearts just as God spoke and breathed life and breath into man at the original creation. At conversion, God's Spirit takes the spiritual man and recreates him in his own image.

SUFFICIENCY

"In this new life one's nationality or race or education or social position is unimportant; such things mean nothing. Whether a person has Christ is what matters and he is equally available to all" (3:11). We probably do not know barriers or divisions as strong as the ones existing in the time of Paul. No barrier today—neither the Iron Curtain nor race nor social differences—can even approach the divisions known in the ancient world.

The word "where" (KJV) in this phrase means "in which state," referring to the state in which the soul is being renewed day by day. Paul was saying not only that there is no distinction or division, but also that it is impossible for them to exist. He was saying that it is impossible for the

Spirit of Christ to be growing and maturing in believers while barriers exist that separate them. There should be no distinctions, schisms, or dissension where Christ is Lord and where the sanctification process is going on. Paul said, "In the state I am talking about, it is not only a fact, but also an impossibility for it to be any other way."

Notice the barriers he described: "... neither Greek, nor Jew, circumcision nor uncircumcision, Barbarian, Scythian, bond or free...." (KJV). These were strong barriers and distinctions. We couldn't find two races of people more proud than the Greeks and the Jews. The Greeks thought that anyone who didn't speak Greek was a barbarian, so they wouldn't even study another language. They were the aristocrats of the ancient world. To them, anyone not a Greek was a barbarian.

The Jews weren't much better, saying they were God's chosen people. They looked with disdain on people of every other nationality. Paul was saying, "In Jesus it doesn't matter what your pedigree is or where you were born, whether you are Jew or Greek. In the state where we are growing into Christ's image day by day, there is neither Greek nor Jew, circumcision nor uncircumcision."

The reference to circumcision could mean a number of things. It could either refer to purely religious distinctions or to the fact that those who were Jews prided themselves on their circumcision. It may have referred to the fact that Jewish proselytes who converted to Judaism were still despised because they had not been circumcised in their infancy as the Jews had been. Whatever it means, the distinction doesn't matter in Christ. No matter what the religious background is or how faithful one has been to certain rituals, in Christ we have become one.

"Barbarian, Scythian" was written in succession rather than in opposition. Barbarians were very primitive, crude people. The Scythians were more "barbarian" than the

Barbarians; they were among the most cruel people in the world. Josephus called the Scythians "wild beasts." There was no one who lived more ruthlessly and without conscience, decency, and order than the Scythians.

In Christ we are "neither . . . bond nor free" (KJV). These words appear in opposition. According to Roman law, slaves were not even considered as human beings. They had no rights under the law that controlled the world at that time. They could not marry. The owner could do anything he wanted to with his slave. He could maim, thrash, beat, or kill him. A slave was a living tool. In the ancient world slaves had no fellowship with free men. But Paul says, "In Christ there is neither bond nor free."

Christ is sufficient for all of these distinctions. It doesn't matter where we were born, what nationality we claim, which side of the tracks we live on, what our religious background is, how faithful we have been to ritual and ceremonial religion, how barbaric we have been, whether we are despised or whether we are free. The grace of God gathers us all in.

Nobody is too far away to be reached by God. Nobody is too deep in sin to be changed. Nobody is too far gone to be touched by the Spirit of God. Even the Scythian, that wild beast of the field, could be changed and saved by the grace of God. Then a slave could go to church with his master. The only place where that slave ever amounted to anything was in the fellowship of the church, where his master might sit at his feet and listen to the wisdom God gave him.

There is no distinction in Christ. That is the glory of the Church and the Christian faith. People of all persuasions, all backgrounds, and all cultures are bathed in the blood of Christ. All Christians come under the control of the Holy Spirit, can grow into full knowledge, and mature in the image of Christ.

" . . . But Christ is all, and in all" (3:11, KJV). That meant that Christ is everything we need to be. There is no requirement of grace placed upon me that Christ is not sufficient to produce within me. Every need that we may have in order to grow and mature, Christ can sustain. There is no need to depend upon nationality, religious ceremony, culture, or status. We have nothing to offer except Jesus. All God will ever approve in us is Jesus. He supplies every need.

Paul said also that Christ is *in* all. There are two possible interpretations of that phrase. "All" could be considered a neuter or a masculine word. If it is neuter, it means that Christ permeates all the relationships of life. Every relation we have, he is in it all. If it is masculine, it means that Christ indwells every believer regardless of who he is. Either he permeates every relationship of life or he indwells every believer regardless of his status or class—Greek, Jew, circumcised, uncircumcised, Barbarian, Scythian, bond, or free. He is in all.

These truths are a beautiful witness and a reminder to those of us who often struggle for more, who often seek additional understanding and crave and sometimes pray for more experiences. Paul said that Jesus Christ is everything for every experience of life. It is a reminder to us to find our center and circumference, our joy and delight, in him. It is a reminder to us that in Jesus all the fullness of the Godhead dwells bodily. We worship God by worshiping Jesus. We center on Christ. He is all and in all.

The Christian putting off the old man is not just a matter of stopping certain things. He has put on a new man as a new creation. A genuine change has taken place in his life. It is what Christ, who is all and in all, produces in him. It is what he wants to produce in all of us.

12

Chosen
by God
*Colossians
3:12-16*

"SINCE YOU HAVE BEEN CHOSEN by God who has given you this new kind of life, and because of his deep love and concern for you, you should practice tenderhearted mercy and kindness to others. Don't worry about making a good impression on them but be ready to suffer quietly and patiently" (3:12).

The negative side of the Christian faith means putting away such things as fornication, uncleanness, and inordinate affection. The positive side of commitment is seen in this passage. The word "since" refers to "having put on the new man" in chapter 3, verse 10. In light of the fact that we have put on the new man, certain characteristics should be seen in our lives.

The verb "put on" (KJV), an aorist imperative verb, gives a command, something to be obeyed immediately, without delay, without hesitation. This verb is also tied to "love" in verse 14. Just as we put on the characteristics mentioned in the next verses, so we are to put on love. Love completes the attire of the Christian.

COVENANT

Three things in this passage need to be examined. The first is the word "covenant." "Elect," "holy," and "beloved"

(KJV) are three words which belong to Israel in its covenant relationship with God. These three words, appearing through the Old Testament, applied to God's chosen people. God has chosen Israel; they are an elect people; they are a holy and much loved people.

The Apostle Paul took these three covenant words that speak specifically to Israel and applied them to the Gentile believers. The fact that they were Jewish words used to describe God's chosen people implies that the church in the New Testament is, in some way, the continuation of the covenant people of the Old Testament. Paul used the words that would identify Christian commitment as a covenant relationship.

Being "chosen by God" means that there is not merit due us, but God. We are a peculiar people, who have been placed into a unique relationship with God. Because of this incomparable position as Christians, we need to be reminded of who we are so we will behave better and live more in keeping with our calling.

When we were saved, we entered into that covenant relationship with him. Paul used these three words concerning our being the elect of God, pointing out that we enjoy this incomparable position through faith in Jesus.

The word "holy" (KJV) means "set apart for the purposes of God." "Beloved" (KJV) means that we are the objects of his matchless love, which is part of our covenant relationship also. When he said "holy and beloved," he was reminding them, not of his love but of their position as objects of God's love. Every action God has taken toward us, with us, in us, and through us has been because he loves us and because he wants what is best for us. Because we have entered into this covenant with God and he with us, we can face life knowing that we will never be out of the circumference of his love.

CHARACTERISTICS

Some of the characteristics of the covenant relationship ought to be reflected in our lives. The first one listed is "tenderhearted mercy." In ancient times, this phrase spoke of the seat of intense emotions such as love and hate. We use the word "heart" in the same way, as in "I love you with all my heart." We are to have hearts full of mercy and compassion like Jesus in the Gospels. When the writers told how much Jesus cared for the lame, the blind, the weak, and the widows, he was shown as having a heart full of mercy, compassion, and concern for them.

In our covenant relationship with God, we ought also to have hearts of compassion for each other. Every one of these characteristics listed relates to our attitude toward one another. Other characteristics would be quite legitimate, but notice Paul didn't mention such things as cleverness, creativity, ingenuity, industry, or anything relating to what we could do in our own strength. Every characteristic he mentioned related to others—to the family of God, to the Body. If we aren't right with each other, we are not prepared to go into the world and spread the gospel of Jesus Christ.

The next characteristic is "kindness," which means "being as concerned for our brother's needs as we are for our own." We could possibly fake "a heart of compassion," but a heart that honestly longs to see our brother's needs met just as quickly as our own is something different.

"Humbleness of mind" (KJV), which is mentioned next, is the spirit which places self last. It does not demand its rights, but puts others and God first. Another characteristic is "meekness" (KJV), which means "to accept without murmuring whatever God places in our lives." It means accepting without resistance what evil man may inflict upon us. Whatever is done to us by God or man we meet without resistance, without complaining. "Longsuffering" (KJV) means "patience under provocation, self-restraint when we are tempted to act quickly or severely." A long-suffering person, when tempted, is very patient, even though provoked.

"Be gentle" means, in this context, "a mutual self-control, as two persons, when inclined to fight, mutually draw back and maintain control of themselves."

Those enjoying the covenant relationship are also "forgiving one another" (3:13, KJV). Three Greek words are all translated "forgive" or "forgiveness": *apoluo, aphieemi,* and the less common word, *karizomai,* which comes from the root word, *karis* ("grace"). Paul used this less common word in writing to the Colossians. Such forgiveness is based on grace, which means that the offending person is treated even better than he deserves, just as God treats us better than we deserve when he forgives us.

There are times when the other person has really given us cause to retaliate because we think we have good reason. But "forgiveness" means that we give them not what they deserve, but forgiveness. We forgive them whether they want to be forgiven or not. The initiative in forgiveness comes from us, not the other person. It doesn't matter how he or she acts or what his or her response is. We are to forgive.

The phrase "the Lord forgave you" is aorist tense and refers to something that happened at a point in the past. But "forbearing and forgiving" (KJV) are present tense and refer to continuous action. We began these actions when we committed our lives to God. Jesus forgave us as we committed ourselves to him. But we are continually to be "forbearing with one another, forgiving one another." We never finish doing things that need forbearance and forgiveness.

In the original language "one another" (KJV) could be translated "yourselves." The fellowship and the relationship are so close that when we respond in grace to someone, we are actually responding to ourselves and our own needs. If we don't forgive others, we are inflicting unforgiveness upon ourselves. Our relationship within the Body means we cannot inflict punishment on one portion of the body without hurting all the other parts. Neither can we forgive one part of our body without it affecting all in this corporate sense. Christians are bound together in a fellowship that is eternal and perpetual. There is a tremendous sense of community in God's kingdom. We belong to each other and share in a common origin and common life. We are the Body of Christ.

The phrase "If any man have a quarrel against any..." (3:13, KJV) encourages me because it admits that the early church, like us, had problems with people not getting along. It would be hard for me to see the things I see among Christian people today if I didn't understand that dissension is not new. In the Christian community, there are disagreements that need to be resolved. The fact that we, as the elect, have put on these characteristics means that we continue to love, forbear, and forgive when conflicts, quarrels, and schisms arise.

We forgive others "... even as Christ forgave [us]" (KJV). The ground of our forgiveness is his forgiveness of us. Even if there were justifiable cause for complaint, Paul reminded them that God had a cause for complaint against them too. If someone grieves us, we should remember that our sins are a grievance against God, who forgave us.

We will never have to forgive as much as God forgave us. Moreover, we have all received more forgiveness than we deserve. We have also received more grace than we had a right to expect, so we should be gracious and forgive each other. God places things in our lives for us to give them away. If we want grace, we give grace. If we want forgiveness, we give forgiveness. The things we give away are an indication of what we need to receive. Since God has been gracious and forgiving to us, we have forgiveness to give to someone else. If we can't forgive—if we can't be gracious and kind—then Satan has bound up a precious gift of God.

Being angry, bitter, or hostile hurts only us. But as we forgive and forbear, we release forgiveness and forbearance into the Body. What we give individually is multiplied and spread throughout the Body.

COMPLETION

"Most of all, let love guide your life, for then the whole church will stay together in perfect harmony" (3:14). "Most of all" does not mean that love is more important than all these things. The phrase literally means "over all" or "around all." To be more exact, it speaks of a belt that we place around us to hold our garments in proper place, that which completes or unites our outfit. Love is like that. It makes all of the rest possible, practical, and meaningful.

We could mechanically produce all of the characteristics listed in this passage and no one else might know the truth, but God. But it would inflict a poison into the fellowship of the church unless it is put on with the bond of love. If we don't have the controlling spirit of love encircling, enclosing, and empowering all, then we are not complete.

How do we love? We love God by dwelling on his love for us, being reminded of how much he loved us. Moses wrote, "He didn't choose you and pour out his love upon you because you were a larger nation than any other, for you were the smallest of all! It was just because he loves you, and because he kept his promise to your ancestors. That is why he brought you out of slavery in Egypt with such amazing power and mighty miracles" (Deuteronomy 7:7, 8).

God loved the nation Israel. He chose them for his people. Like them, we are the objects of his love. When we dwell upon that love, God enables us to love in return. We love him and we love each other. The moving, motivating characteristic of the Church, that which completes it all, that which gives meaning and purpose to it all, is love.

FREEDOM IN THE LORD

"Let the peace of heart which comes from Christ be always present in your hearts and lives, for this is your responsibility and privilege as members of his body. And always be thankful" (3:15).

The peace of Christ is the peace which Christ imparts. When we come into an experience with Jesus Christ, he imparts or transfers peace to us. It was the legacy he left the Church. "I am leaving you with a gift—peace of mind and heart! And the peace I give isn't fragile like the peace the world gives. So don't be troubled or afraid" (John 14:27).

When there is no peace in our hearts, it means something has caused us to be estranged from our Lord. Where Jesus is in control, where he is in evidence, there is peace.

"Let the peace . . . be always present" is in the imperative mood. The King James Version reads, "Let the peace . . . rule. . . ." It is not an option, but an imperative, a command.

We don't make peace rule in our hearts. We let it rule. If we are disobedient to God, rebellious, and out of fellowship, we keep God's peace from ruling in our hearts. We need to give diligence to those things that keep us walking with him, in obedience, submissiveness, and strength.

The word "rule" means "to umpire" or "arbitrate." When differences arise, the peace of God is the umpire, the one who calls the shots, or makes the decisions. This certainly applies to individual hearts, but Paul was primarily talking to the Church. Whenever there is a difference of opinion, a divisive matter which arises within the body, the peace of God is to be the umpire. Every dissension, every schism, every concern, and every difference must come under the peace of Christ ruling in our hearts.

Strife is the inevitable result of being out of fellowship with God. Whenever we walk in harmony with God, there is a unity, a oneness. Whenever we are out of harmony with God, there come all sorts of dissension, strife, and division. It is encouraging to know that the New Testament church had its differences, too. As we have that difficulty in common, we also share the solution.

"Let the peace of Christ rule in your heart. For this is your responsibility and privilege as members of his body." Paul was talking about the nature of our relationship in the body of Christ. There are some parts of our bodies for which we haven't discovered a real function, but there is nothing superfluous about our bodies. God made us with nothing extra. Everything was necessary and important. Each member of the body has a function to perform. If we are to be healthy, it is important for every member of our bodies to function as intended.

God has gone to great lengths to compare the Christian community with a body. Throughout the New Testament we are called "the Body of Christ." Paul particularly wrote of our being members of one body. Peter wrote about our being "living stones built into the temple of God." In a physical body, every member is important. And if the body is to be healthy and happy, every member needs to function in its designated place.

The same is true spiritually. Any part of the Body of Christ that doesn't function or tries to function as another part ends up harming the Body. Paul said, "See to it that the peace of Christ rules in your heart because you have been called into one body." Disunity of the Body is incompatible with peace in the hearts of individual members.

"And always be thankful" seems almost an afterthought. Some translate this phrase, "Don't fail to be grateful." It could also be translated, "Become thankful." Paul was saying that thankfulness needs to be cultivated. It is not natural for us to be grateful. None of us, as members of the

Body, is independent. It is vital that we maintain harmony, moving in unity together. To do so we must cultivate the spirit of gratitude.

This command to be grateful, some think, means that we ought to cultivate an attitude of gratefulness only toward God. That is certainly part of it. But Paul seemed also to say that we need to look for things in each other for which to be grateful. A spirit of gratitude promotes harmony. If we look at each other with a desire to determine and discover things that can make us grateful for each other, it insures that the peace of God will serve as an umpire or arbitrator in our lives.

"Let the word of Christ dwell in you richly in all wisdom . . ." (KJV). "The word of Christ" does not just refer to the words Christ spoke on earth as recorded in the Gospels. The phrase refers to the Word revealed through all the New Testament writers, through the Gospels, the Acts, and the letters that were being circulated. We are to let the Word—which Christ revealed through those whom he inspired—dwell in us richly.

The word "dwell" means "to settle down and be at home, as in a permanent dwelling place." The Word of Christ ought to make its home in our lives. When the teachings of Christ and the Word of God as revealed in Christ come into our lives, they should be comfortable. The Word of Christ ought to be compatible with the way we live. If anyone in the world ought to live the way God says, it is God's people. Paul said, "Be sure that the Word of God finds a permanent place to live in you."

The phrase "enrich your lives and make you wise" suggests that the Word of God dwelling in us will produce a wealth of meaning and power. "Wise" means "the ability to apply truth and teaching to our lives to make us better people."

To be sure that the Word dwells in us, we must be obedient to what it says. We cannot know what it says if we don't read it, nor can we be obedient to it if we don't make prayer and submissiveness a daily part of our experience. We must attend to the Word so that when God reveals truth to us, we may do it. Our problem today is that many of us know things we ought to do but aren't doing. Our arrogance, pride, selfishness, and self-sufficiency keep us from being obedient to Christ. All of us know more than we are putting into practice. The problem is not ignorance or lack of understanding, but that we are not always willing to do what we know to do. Hence, God can't reveal himself more deeply to us until we are obedient to what we already know.

Part of the church's responsibility is "teaching and admonishing" (KJV). "Teaching" is the positive aspect of imparting and declaring the truth. "Admonishing" has both a positive and a negative aspect—the idea of warning, reproof, or rebuke; it also has the positive side of encouraging.

Paul said to teach and to admonish: " . . . in psalms and hymns and spiritual songs." Throughout his writings, Paul gave an order of service with worship in music as a major part. We are not just singing songs, but worshiping with our songs of praise. In olden times, it was not unusual to preach by singing. It was one of the techniques of teaching, or instructing.

We teach and admonish one another in three kinds of songs. The word "psalms" literally means "any song set to music." One may ask, "How can there be a song not set to music?" Poetry would be an illustration, something not necessarily having melody. A psalm also means "truth set to melody." Many of the songs which the early church sang were the psalms of David.

"Hymns" means "poems sung in order to praise God." They were songs some of the Christians composed, sometimes spontaneously, and sung in praise to God.

"Spiritual songs" were songs spiritual in nature. It is

possible for some songs to have all three characteristics. It is important for a song to be doctrinally sound, or in keeping with divine revelation. Music is not superfluous, something to use just to warm up a congregation for the preaching. Preaching is not the only thing God wants us to do in church. We will never understand the place of music until we understand it as a form of worship. As we sing, we are leading in praise to God and in a real sense are preaching, teaching, and admonishing each other with the eternal truth of God.

We are to "sing with grace in our hearts" (KJV). The obvious meaning is that we are to sing with our hearts as well as our lips, not just going through the motions or saying the words, but singing from our hearts. To sing with grace in our hearts means we have a conscious understanding of our need of God's presence in our lives.

The original language says, "singing with *the* grace in your hearts," referring to the grace of God, the grace provided by and nurtured by the Holy Spirit.

We are to sing "to the Lord." A common idea today of the sole purpose of worship is the edification of the believer. Worship, however, should be unto God. When worship is directed to God, it will edify the believer, but the primary goal of worship is not our own edification. We come to church, sit with our Bibles, and wait for the preacher to feed us, but that is not the purpose of worship. When someone leaves saying, "I didn't get a thing out of that sermon," he came for the wrong reason. We don't come to get something out of worship; we come to add something.

Praise edifies. It builds and releases God's power. As we genuinely worship, his principles come alive in us. We should ask ourselves the next time we feel we didn't get anything from the service, "What did I bring to it?" If we are simply spectators, then we make those leading the service performers or entertainers with the responsibility of pleasing us. Let us not make church like everything else. We come together to praise God, for it is in our praise to him that we find our edification, strength, and motivation. If we seek our own edification first, we miss everything. We are challenged, and our emotions are churned, but we leave the service no different. If we come to church to praise God, no one can rob us of that privilege.

13

God's
Ideal
Family
Colossians
3:17—4:1

"AND WHATEVER YOU DO OR SAY, let it be as a representative of the Lord Jesus, and come with him into the presence of God the Father to give him your thanks" (3:17).

Not only do we praise God in worship and singing, but every word and thought can be transformed into genuine worship of God. The principles given to us for praise, worship, and commitment extend even more practically in the relationships of life.

The next passage deals with relationships within the home, which can also be used as a basis for praising God. Christianity added no new element to the family. Many years before Christ came, Aristotle spoke of three pairs of relationships absolutely essential in society: husband and wife, parent and child, and master and servant. Many years before Christ, the elements of the home were already established. Christianity proposed no new guidelines because all through the ages, the home has been guided by two simple principles: authority and obedience. Christianity introduced no new principles but a new presence into the home—the presence of God himself.

The Christian home is perhaps the greatest contribution, practically speaking, that Christianity has made to the world. The introduction of this new power glorified, brightened, and transfigured relationships within the home.

ATTITUDE

"And whatever you do or say, let it be as a representative of Jesus Christ." The imperative verb, though not implicit, is implied. Everything we do, think, and say should be done in the name of the Lord Jesus Christ. We apply the rule of the presence of Christ to everything we do. We allow Christianity to affect how we live, act, react, relate, work, love, and obey. Christianity is involved in everything we say and do, in all the relationships of life.

"... Do all in the name of the Lord Jesus" (KJV). The name of Christ represents the person and presence of Christ. To live in the name of Christ means that we live in identification with him. We recognize his will and authority over us in all our relationships and activities. We acknowledge that in everything we are dependent upon him. We live under his control and power and in his spirit and presence. It means that we live conscious of him every day.

"Do all... giving thanks to God and the Father by him..." (3:17, KJV). Gratitude, as Paul mentioned earlier, is to be an important part of our lives. We spend too much of our time complaining about what we don't have and talking about our rights. The truth is that if we got what we deserve, we would never see another day. We would go through the anguish and agony of hell, now and hereafter, for that is what we deserve.

Thanking God in times of disappointment or discouragement is, in effect, praising God and trusting God that we have the victory in the midst of those times.

Verse 17 is a transitional thought. Many commentators believe the verse goes with the preceding passage rather than with this specific instruction for the Christian home.

It is logical to assume that the message of this verse applies to both of these passages.

"You wives, submit yourselves to your husbands, for that is what the Lord has planned for you. And you husbands must be loving and kind to your wives and not bitter against them, nor harsh" (3:18). The principles of authority are clear. The words "submit to your husbands" are not referring to all women being in subjection to all men but to Christian wives and husbands in the marriage relationship. It is obvious Paul was writing to born-again believers. There is no intimation in this verse or anywhere else in Scripture that the subjection is based on inferiority, intelligence, morality, spirituality, worth, value, integrity, or anything. It refers only to a relationship of authority within the family. That is all. It is absolutely essential that we understand who the authority figure is in the home. If we do not accept it in the home, we will not accept it out of the home. If we do not accept it in the home, we will have difficulty with God, who is the ultimate authority, and with the police, the government. Authority is to be learned in the home.

"For that is what the Lord has planned for you." The verb tense used in the original language, implies that it was not a temporary or recent circumstance that brought this about. It has always been God's plan, the way God designed it. When Adam and Eve were created, they were equal. Yet God placed Eve in a position of subjection and submission to Adam. It has always been so.

"And you husbands must be loving and kind to your wives and not bitter against them, nor harsh" (3:19). In the Roman Empire and under Jewish law, a woman was a thing, a possession with no legal rights. Only under extreme circumstances of great cruelty or immorality was the wife given any rights of divorce. Under those ancient laws, the husband had all the privileges and rights; the wife had all the responsibilities and the duties. Into such a world

Jesus Christ came. The New Testament message is "Husbands, love your wives." For the first time it was revealed that there is to be a reciprocal obligation in the home. It was not just a matter of the wife submitting to the husband and the husband having all the rights and privileges. There was to be give and take—the wife showing submission and the husband giving love.

Perfect love controls and transforms all exercise of authority. If a husband loves his wife with *agape* love—the unselfish, sacrificing, undying kind of love that God has for us—tyranny, unkindness, selfishness, and cruelty cannot exist. It removes from submission everything the wife might feel is distasteful and difficult. It actually places the husband in a position of true subjection, for he is compelled by love to fulfill every claim which the wife may make upon him for support, sympathy, protection, and happiness. It is her submission to him and his love for her that results in mutual subjection and submission.

In other places in the New Testament, we are told to submit ourselves to one another. A true love relationship makes it impossible for the husband not to respond to the wife and provide for her. He must do it because he is driven by love. He is willing to give his life for her and to do anything necessary for her happiness. In reality, he too is in submission to her.

"And be not bitter, . . ." the husband was exhorted. The word "bitter" means "harsh and unfeeling." Love makes it impossible to be bitter. A wife never need fear acknowledging her husband's authority if she is sure of his love. Her attitude of submission will make it easier for him to love as he ought.

The greatest assault of Satan in our time is coming upon the Christian home. Many who have contemplated divorce and seriously considered the break-up of their homes, are respected people in their community, those who hold high office or position in their church and have the esteem of their peers. But the pressure, hurt, and tension are there, along with despair.

Christian husbands must love their wives. Christian wives must submit themselves to their husbands. All must quit thinking of themselves and do what God has told them to do. There are complications that come when one partner is a Christian and the other is not, but the principles are the same. If the Church is to have the impact upon the world it ought to have, there must be a recommitment of Christian homes to what God wants them to be.

"You children must always obey your fathers and mothers, for that pleases the Lord" (3:20). Immediately, someone may question whether a child should obey his parents if the parents are wrong, or if they ask children to do something that is wrong. The truth is, that seldom happens. This exhortation is given in the context of doing everything in the name of the Lord. Human authority is never absolute. Whenever there is a conflict between what human authority says to do and what God says to do, we have no choice but to do what God says. But God has given children to parents who also have special responsibilities. Responsibility without authority is unthinkable.

The word "obey" comes from a word meaning "hearken at the door," or "answer the door." It refers to one who responds to a knock on the door and then listens to the message delivered. Children listen to the counsel, advice, and commands of their parents. As God's children, we listen to him and do what he requests.

"That [obedience] pleases the Lord . . . ." because such an attitude accepts the biblical standard. It pleases God when we obey him. In the world in which Christianity was born, children had no rights. The law of the father's power in the Roman Empire was absolute. A father could sell his children into slavery or do anything he chose to do with them. He could beat, maim and even sentence them to death, carrying out the order with no one saying a word. He had absolute authority. Into that world came the Christian message for children to obey their parents in all things, for it is "well-pleasing unto the Lord" (KJV).

Paul continued, "Fathers, don't scold your children so much that they become discouraged and quit trying" (3:21). Again there is a reciprocal responsibility. The child is to be obedient to the parent, but the parent is also to be understanding and compassionate toward the child. The word "fathers" is neuter and could refer to both fathers and mothers, as it does in other usages. More than likely, it refers primarily to the father since he has already been designated as the authority in the home. Since children must obey, then parents must be on guard lest they discourage their children by unreasonable demands. Literally, it says, "Don't be continually irritating your children," or habitually provoking them. Parents need to understand that if they are the means through which God brings children into the world, then parents have a special responsibility to their children. It is unthinkable that parents could be callous toward their children. Rather than continually provoking our children, we should be concerned for them.

The one thing I most cherished about my father was that he was always there. Whenever I needed him, he was there. Now that he has been gone these many years, there are still times that I need him and he is still there by way of the principles and habits he instilled in me. That was his responsibility and became his fulfillment, joy. We have the same opportunity with our children.

Discipline and encouragement are both needed. We need to be careful that we don't try to make our children act like adults before they are ready. Perhaps the world would be better off if we acted more like children ourselves sometimes, especially in the simplicity of faith. We must not make children grow up too quickly. They will not understand what we are trying to teach, but will understand our attitudes. If we are hostile, they will pick up our hostility. Some parents are reaping the results of their own critical tongues. They shouldn't be surprised if they are continually provoking and irritating their children if the children rebel against authority. We have a responsibility under God not to provoke our children. We must discipline them, but we must also encourage them. They must know that discipline is for their best interest.

If our homes were what they should be, we would avoid spending a lot of money for doctor bills, medication, and counseling. Most spouses who have nervous breakdowns are not having good relations with their partner. When parents have problems with their children, and children with their parents, it is often because both sides are not in proper relationship to each other. If we applied what God has said, it would revolutionize the home and all of life.

LIVING UNTO THE LORD

"You slaves must always obey your earthly masters, not only trying to please them when they are watching you but all the time; obey them willingly because of your love for the Lord and because you want to please him" (3:22).

It is easy for us to keep principles in the abstract. When we get down to specifics and particulars, it gets more difficult. The Apostle Paul got down to specifics in this passage.

In the previous verses, Paul applied the truth of living "unto the Lord" to the home. He next discussed the relationship of servant to master, which in that day was an extension of household life. In our day the same principles would certainly apply to relationships of employee to employer, as well as to other interpersonal relationships.

Paul laid down first the principle of obedience, responsibility, and personal integrity in the relationship of slaves to masters. The New Testament does not specifically attack or even suggest the abolition of slavery. However, the Bible lays down principles that ultimately make it impossible for slavery as we know it to exist. If a master treats a slave as a brother in Christ and as an equal in the sight of the Lord, and if a slave treats his master as one given to him in authority by the Lord, the relationship would not be recognized as slavery as it existed in the ancient world. Indeed, the gospel of Jesus Christ is the principal reason that slavery no longer exists today.

Many relationships are simply not just or fair, but Paul was saying that in whatever relationship we find ourselves, there are some principles that should be applied to it. Paul did not obliterate earthly distinctions. He told the slaves to be conscientious workers. Christianity has never offered anyone an escape from hard work. In fact, Christianity will enable a hard worker to work harder. It will challenge a person to give his best, to work to his full capacity. It challenges him to rise above the ordinary, the average, and the mediocre and to excel.

The restlessness in the human heart that calls us to seek, to press on, and to achieve is a call from God. God has planted that motivation in our hearts. Christianity does not remove us from difficult situations. Instead, it teaches us how to respond in the midst of difficult situations.

"Always obey your earthly masters." There were no conditions or exceptions. The only exception might be where the master commanded the slave to do something that was sinful or against God. The Lord is to be the ultimate authority. But unless there is a conflict between what God says and what we are instructed to do, we are to do it. The Christian slave was not at liberty to choose when and where he would be obedient. We need to understand the principle of obedience to authority. There is also a principle of excellence and responsibility.

Paul described such service by saying, "... not with eye

service" (KJV). "Eye service" means "the kind of work we do when the boss is watching, when we know someone is looking over our shoulders." In other words, we do a good job when no one is watching or even if no one seems to care or even if there were no rewards or praise. Work done just to please those who have instructed us is a very poor incentive. To do a job just to please the one who has asked for it to be done becomes a burden and a duty. If we apply this principle to life, we will not be obedient just when we are being watched, for we will do it as "unto the Lord."

We are to work "in singleness of heart" (KJV). "Singleness" means "purity" or "sincerity," the opposite of double-dealing and hypocrisy. We are to have a sincerity of purpose, working out the principles of obedience, diligence, and faithfulness in all our relationships. We are to do our work "because of [our] love for the Lord."

The whole passage is described within the circumference of God's will, presence, and purposes for our lives. We are to relate to each other and apply these principles as "unto the Lord."

God's prescribed way of loving and serving each other is to do what we do, not to please men or because we are being observed, but because of the sincerity and purity of our hearts.

PATTERN

"And whatsoever ye do, do it heartily, as to the Lord, and not unto men" (3:23, KJV). The word "whatsoever" means that no matter how little, mundane, insignificant, or inconsequential something seems to be, it is all to be done heartily.

The word "do" appears twice in this passage, but is translated from two different words. The first is just the simple verb "to do." The second one is a more complex, more descriptive word, which speaks of labor, toil, and diligence. The word "heartily" literally means "out of the soul." Whatever task we accept, whatever job we set out to do, whatever assignment is given to us, we are to do it diligently, enthusiastically, with all our heart and soul.

A lazy, slothful professing Christian is a great discredit to the cause of Christ. He is inconsistent with the pattern of the New Testament. Any theology that causes us to sit down and fold our hands is heresy. Today lethargy, apathy, and laziness grip God's people who only want to be fed, cared for, and ministered to. But aren't we called not to be ministered to, but to minister? There must be diligence, effort, and activity. Laziness, idleness, and lack of diligence, and dedication are incompatible and inconsistent with both the truth of Jesus Christ and the principles of the New Testament.

When we apply the principle of diligence in our lives, we are not working for pay, for selfish ambition, or for the pleasure of our earthly bosses or masters. We accept tasks to be done so that we can offer our service *to the Lord.* The rewards that God gives to the diligent, to those who are open for his use, will be taken and laid again at his feet. That puts work in a whole new perspective. We do the unpleasant things because we are doing them as to the Lord. When we have the right attitude toward work, the place where we make our living will become an altar of sacrifice and a place of dedication to the Lord.

PROMISE

Then Paul spoke of the promise. "... Remembering that it is the Lord Christ who is going to pay you, giving you your full portion of all he owns. He is the one you are really working for. And if you don't do your best for him, he will pay you in a way that you won't like—for he has no special favorites who can get away with shirking" (3:24, 25). By Roman law, slaves had no rights of possession. They could not hold property. A slave was completely owned by someone else. Yet, here Paul wrote that they would receive their "full portion" from the Lord. Slaves with no rights and no possessions were being made yet heirs of eternity, heirs of God. What a promise to those slaves who were deemed valueless in the Roman world! What a tremendous joy for them to hear the Apostle Paul say, "In Christ you will receive your inheritance in the Lord. The earthly master may not treat you well. He may not remember to thank you. There may be no rewards here, but God is watching and he won't forget."

Paul wrote: "He is the one you are really working for." Sometimes the earthly demands placed on us obscure that truth. Sometimes we do not get the response, the reward we would like, from earthly relationships. But, we serve the Lord Christ. Sometimes when we face points of conflict and pressure in earthly relationships, it is because God is proving us to see if we really do serve him.

The last portion of that promise appears as a warning. "He that doeth wrong shall receive for the wrong which he hath done" (3:25, KJV). Does it refer to the master who is unjust, or does it refer to the slave who might not be a diligent, conscientious slave? In reality, it refers to both.

The slave might think that his master gets preferential treatment or he may think that because he was a slave on earth, God will overlook his faults and excuse him for some of the wrong things he had done. The truth is that God "has no special favorites who can get away with shirking."

God is absolutely impartial. None of us will have God in debt to us. God judges on the basis of what is right, never on the basis of some superficial consideration. God is going to judge according to the heart, according to reality and truth.

If wives are not right in their relationship to their husbands, wives will receive the fruit of what they have sown. God is no respecter of persons. If husbands don't love their wives and are not right in their relationship, husbands will receive that which they have sown, for God is no respecter of persons.

If parents are not the kind of parents they ought to be, and if they discourage and provoke their children and don't provide for them as they ought, parents will reap what they have sown, for God is no respecter of persons. If children do not obey their parents and respect and love them in the Lord, children will receive the fruit of what they have sown, for God is no respecter of persons.

If slaves have not been conscientious and diligent, active and determined, busy and energetic in every way in their service, slaves will reap what they have sown, for God is no respecter of persons. If masters have been unjust in dealing with those who are under them, they, too, will reap what they have sown. God is no respecter of persons. "He that doeth wrong shall receive for the wrong which he hath done" (KJV).

There is the promise of inheritance, blessing, and reward. Along with that is the promise of judgment by God upon us all. We all fit into this relationship somewhere. The Apostle Paul challenged us to do whatever we do in life as "unto the Lord."

When I understood that truth as a teenager, I became a straight *A* student. I wasn't especially smart. It just dawned on me that what I did in the classroom reflected on Christ and my Savior. I began to study, listen, and prepare myself as "unto the Lord."

This truth affects every area of life. Whatever assignment we have, be it as husband or wife, as employer or employee, or as minister or laity, we must do it as "unto the Lord." What we do, we do for God, representing him. Our actions, diligence, and responsiveness are a direct reflection upon him. We cannot live one way and believe another. We must do the truth.

We live under his observation and presence. Whatever we do, wherever we go, he is there and we are to do that which he assigned to us as unto him. We have built a subculture of honors in the Church today that often conflicts with what we know about God's method of reward. We like the places of honor because honor of men feeds our egos. But that isn't proper motivation for any kind of Christian service. There would be no shortage of people to share Christ, of people to sing in the choir, or of people to go from door to door sharing the Word of God, if we did what we do as "unto the Lord." In every relationship in and out of the church organization itself, we have assignments, responsibilities, influence, and opportunities. Paul said that whatever we do, we must do it with our hearts and souls as "unto the Lord," for we serve the Lord Jesus Christ.

MASTERS

"You slave owners must be just and fair to all your slaves. Always remember that you, too, have a Master in heaven who is closely watching you" (4:1).

Verse 1 is actually the concluding thought of the passage in chapter 3. Paul dealt with the responsibility of masters, those who own slaves or are in a position of importance, power, and prestige. They are to be very sure that they give their servants what is just and equal. The word "give" (KJV) means "to give out of your own resources," to give what is yours to give. It means to give of yourself, your spirit, your heart. Paul was not saying that everyone ought to have the same position of equality in society. Rather, he was saying that they ought to treat one another with brotherly equality since they are in Christ. He stated in the preceding passage that in Christ there is neither bond nor free.

To the masters Paul was saying, "Be sure you don't lord it over people. Don't get carried away with the sense of your own importance, authority, and power. Give to your servants what is just and equal. Give them the consideration and compassion due Christian brethren."

Paul reminded them that they "too, have a Master in heaven." This principle of the Lordship of Christ is one that would fit every category he had already talked about. In every relationship we enjoy—husband-wife, parent-child, or employer-employee—we must remember that we have "a Master in heaven." The Christian lives under lordship, in submission to his will. We are never justified in basing our actions or our reactions on the attitudes or actions of other people around us, for we are accountable and responsible to God. Someday we will give an account of ourselves to him.

We are children of God, but in another sense we are servants of the Lord Jesus Christ. The favorite phrase of Paul throughout all of his epistles is that he was a slave, a servant of Jesus Christ. He normally called himself either an apostle or a servant or both. A servant was one who was accountable to his master.

The word "servant" speaks of one who is bound to his master until death. When Christ freed us from the bondage of sin, we entered into a relationship of servitude to him in which he is our Lord. Only death can break that bond. Since he lives and never dies, we are never free from our relationship with the Lord. We are his servants eternally.

14
Prayer
and Our
Testimony
Colossians
4:2-7

WE DO NOT SEEM to attach as much significance to prayer today as Paul did. Prayer was very important in the life of the early church, judging from Paul's frequent references to it. It was very much a part of the scriptural commands to the Church itself.

Notice how Paul described the prayer that was to characterize their lives. "Don't be weary in prayer; keep at it" speaks of a constant, careful dedication and diligence. There should be special seasons of prayer when we present special needs to the Lord. Prayer at times ought to be the foremost thing in our minds. For us, prayer is often a very casual exercise, informal, and often not a matter of urgency. But Paul's description of what prayer should be is that it is something we practice steadfastly and persistently.

After telling of how Jesus gave the model prayer, Luke wrote, "Then, teaching them more about prayer, he used this illustration: 'Suppose you went to a friend's house at midnight, wanting to borrow three loaves of bread. You would shout up to him, "A friend of mine has just arrived for a visit and I've nothing to give him to eat." He would call down from his bedroom, "Please don't ask me to get up. The door is locked for the night and we are all in bed. I just can't help you this time" ' " (Luke 1:5-7).

In those days, most of the homes had just one room, so at bedtime people really bedded down for the night. For a man to get up and answer the door meant that he would have to step over all of his children and disturb the whole household.

"But I'll tell you this—though he won't do it as a friend, if you keep knocking long enough he will get up and give you everything you want—just because of your persistence. And so it is with prayer—keep on asking and you will keep on getting; keep on looking and you will keep on finding; knock and the door will be opened" (Luke 11:8, 9).

Paul was saying, "Don't be weary in praying; stay at it. Don't give up." God doesn't always answer our prayers in a second or in a night or a day or a week or a month or even a year. But stay at it! The person who prays as Paul suggested is persistent. His is the kind of praying that Jacob did when he wrestled with the angel in prayer and petition to God, saying he would not let go until the angel blessed him.

Our prayer lives do not know that kind of importunity, that kind of tireless commitment that they ought to have. Some people would be embarrassed to answer the question, "How much time to you spend praying for your worship services each week?" Many pastors spend more time writing and studying than they do praying. We don't really give the time to prayer that it deserves. Most of us would never fall asleep praying because we don't pray long enough to fall asleep.

Prayerlessness on our part could be interpreted as our determination that we do not need God to do anything for us. As long as we think we can do something ourselves, we won't pray. Lack of prayer is an indication of a lack of trust or confidence in God. We desperately need to pray because prayer is an expression of our helplessness before God.

"Watch for God's answers and remember to be thankful when they come" (4:2). Sin makes us careless, and the carelessness is never more clearly seen than in our prayer life. The word "watch" means "to be awake," "to be alert." It speaks of guarding our minds against wandering thoughts. We have all, on occasion, tried to pray and found ourselves thinking about everything under the sun. We can always count on our minds wandering when we really try to pray. Satan at a time like this becomes very active. Sometimes blasphemous thoughts or a pressing business or personal matter comes into our thoughts. We should give ourselves constantly to prayer, guarding against wandering thoughts.

We must remember that we are in spiritual warfare, as Paul said in Ephesians: "For we are not fighting against people made of flesh and blood, but against persons without bodies—the evil rulers of the unseen world, those mighty satanic beings and great evil princes of darkness who rule this world; and against huge numbers of wicked spirits in the spirit world . . . .

"Pray all the time. Ask God for anything in line with the Holy Spirit's wishes. Plead with him, reminding him of your needs, and keep praying earnestly for all Christians everywhere" (Ephesians 6:12, 18).

We just cannot separate prayer and gratitude. As we think over what God has done for us and we are grateful for what he has done, gratitude becomes the basis of our praying, reminding us of the good things of God. It is very important that we combine prayer with gratitude. Most of the Apostle Paul's prayers started with: "I thank God for . . . ."

Paul was in prison, but he was not praying for his own comfort. Notice that he said, "Pray for us"; the "us" referred to Tychicus, Onesimus, Aristarchus, and those who were with him. He was praying and asking the church to pray that God would bless those who were ministering the Word.

PROCLAMATION

Paul asked for prayer "... that God will give us many chances to preach the Good News of Christ for which I am here in jail. Pray that I will be bold enough to tell it freely and fully, and make it plain, as, of course, I should" (4:3, 4). The apostle used a word for "jail" that indicated he was under house arrest, close supervision. He was in "bonds" (KJV).

Some scholars believe that Paul was thinking of all the churches he had established and of the new frontiers where he wanted to present the gospel. They think he was also asking the church to pray that he would be released so he could freely preach the gospel elsewhere. Perhaps he was praying for his release. If so, then obviously it was so he could preach the gospel, the message of Jesus Christ. He had a one-track heart, with only one direction to go, one message to declare. Jesus Christ was the heart of his message. He said, "For I decided that I would speak only of Jesus Christ and his death on the cross" (1 Corinthians 2:2).

It may be that Paul was also praying and asking they pray that God would give him the ability to communicate the gospel beyond any natural understanding or natural ability. It may be that he wanted them to pray so that when he preached, God would take his words and multiply them far beyond anything he could do and that God would prepare the hearts of the hearers so that they would listen more intently and respond. This prayer is common to his other epistles. To the Corinthians he wrote, "... for there is a wide open door for me to preach and teach here. So much is happening, but there are many enemies" (1 Corinthians 16:9). When we faithfully proclaim the message of Christ, we can also count on many adversaries.

This was not an unusual request from Paul. On other occasions, he had talked about an open door to preach the gospel. He wanted the Colossians also to pray that he would be able to preach.

God forbid that our prayers should center on what we are going to build or buy or do in our church programs. As we pray that God would give us an open door, let it be for the furtherance of the preaching of the gospel of Jesus Christ. That is the reason the·church exists, the reason God has given us the blessings and challenges—to proclaim the message of Jesus Christ. We are not part of what God is doing if we are not a part of that proclamation, part of sharing Christ through personal witness and testimony and through preaching and teaching the gospel.

Christianity cannot be radiated—it has to be communicated. It has to be shared. Pray that we will have an open door of utterance "to speak the mystery of Christ" (KJV), Paul said. The phrase, "mystery of Christ" throughout the New Testament and especially in the epistles of Paul referred to that aspect of the gospel revealed to the Gentiles. The Jews had first assumed that the gospel was exclusively theirs.· But the Apostle Paul said, "God has appointed me an apostle to the Gentiles to tell them the good news of the gospel," which at one time seemed hidden to the Gentile world. Now the covering has been removed and the darkness that hindered the understanding of the truth has also been taken away so that the gospel could be revealed to all people, not just Jews.

The message God has planted in our hearts is that God loves all people and nations. He loves all sinners, regardless of the depths or the nature of their sin.

Paul prayed that God would give him an open door to preach this good news. Paul, being imprisoned, had to pray for an open door. We, however, have many opportunities and seem to take such little advantage of them. No one hinders or forbids us to declare the message of Jesus Christ. No law keeps us from visiting our neighbors to declare the unsearchable riches of Christ. We live in a land where the gospel can be freely proclaimed, but Paul was bound.

Though bound, he continued to pray for liberty to be able to declare the mystery of Christ. We should return to that kind of fervent, continual, diligent prayer that God would give us utterance to speak.

WALKING IN WISDOM

Make the most of your chances to tell others the Good News. Be wise in all your contacts with them. Let your conversation be gracious as well as sensible, for then you will have the right answer for everyone" (4:5, 6).

Paul spoke of how we are to relate to the world, to people who are not saved, and of how we are to measure up to God's image in the eyes of the world. The verses are simple; the admonitions are brief and clear.

Sometimes we spend a great deal of time planning and caring for relationships with each other within our families, and that is all appropriate and right. We ought also to take great care to protect our relationships with believers. Nothing ought to come in the way of God's Spirit moving freely among us. But in this passage the Apostle Paul mentioned the great responsibility believers have in relating to those *outside* the faith.

WALKING

We are to "walk in wisdom toward them that are without, redeeming the time" (4:5, KJV). "Them that are without" literally means "those outside of the church, people of the world who haven't accepted the gospel." The word "walk" means "to order our behavior, the conduct of our lives." We are to conduct our lives in wisdom, referring back to an earlier statement: "For this cause we also, since the day we heard it, do not cease to pray for you, and to desire that you might be filled with the knowledge of his will in all wisdom"

(1:9, KJV). Paul meant that they were to conduct their lives in light of the knowledge of God's will.

All wisdom should lead us to be obedient to God's will. Walking in wisdom means our behavior is to be determined by the will of God, that we are to know the purpose, intent, and plan of God for our lives.

That was why Epaphras, who was one of them according to Paul, was "always earnestly praying for you, asking God to make you strong and perfect and to help you know his will in everything you do" (4:12). This verse places great emphasis on our discerning God's will for our lives. Peter says that it is not God's will that any perish but that all come to repentance (2 Peter 3:9). We could therefore say that it is the will of God that all should come to repentance. If that is the will of God, and if we walk in wisdom, there should be times in our lives set aside to share the gospel of Jesus Christ with the world. If it is the will of God that we love and concern ourselves with the needs of the lost, then we should be concerned.

There is no scriptural ground for apathy on the part of Christians in God's plan for those outside the church. We draw the circle of our friends and our close associates within the fellowship, but we must be careful that we don't draw the circle smaller than God designs. It is the will of God that the gospel be communicated through man, that the lost be reached by the preaching and sharing of the gospel. Our task is to determine what God's will is for us.

Every individual is unique. God described us corporately as members of a body, meaning that the Church is made up of many parts, with many different functions. As part of the Body, we have different gifts with which to minister. If that is true inside, it is true outside. There may be a thousand expressions of Christian concern and a thousand different patterns or styles of Christian witnessing, but we should know what God's will for us is. We must walk in that wisdom toward those outside.

The phrase "redeeming the time" could be translated "purchasing the time" or "buying up the time," meaning "to use the time well." We all have the same amount of time, but some of us get more done than others because we use our time more wisely than others. To redeem the time means to be always on the lookout for an opportunity.

The church is constantly giving opportunities to its members to teach, sing, preach, witness, share, and minister. Yet there are many who deliberately turn down those opportunities.

The time that should be used for God can easily be relinquished to Satan. It can happen in the wink of an eye—when we are praying, when a blasphemous thought or an evil temptation comes into our minds. The precious moment of prayer can be lost so quickly. We are to use the time we have wisely, and be scrupulous with every moment. If we are not careful, we could waste time by putting garbage into our minds by way of television, movies, the radio, the newspapers. If we are to redeem the time, there will be no casual moments, but a constant vigilance.

At least four times in the Bible we read the expression "It is time" or "The time is" relative to redeeming the time. "... The important thing to remember is that our remaining time is very short [and so are our opportunities for doing the Lord's work]" (1 Corinthians 7:29). Those things which we take for granted, the opportunities to love, to express appreciation, to share, to establish friendships, and to build relationships, are so soon gone. The time is short.

"Another reason for right living is this: you know how late it is; time is running out. Wake up, for the coming of the Lord is nearer now than when we first believed" (Romans 13:11). God's people are pictured as being asleep. It reminds us of Rip Van Winkle, who went to sleep one day and years later awakened, having slept through a whole revolution. He didn't even recognize the world he woke up in. One wonders how many Christians are sleeping through the revolutionary changes going on in our world, through some of the greatest days in history.

"For now is the time to seek the Lord, that he may come and shower salvation upon you" (Hosea 10:12). If we are to redeem the time, we must seek the Lord and make him the center of our hearts. We talk about, anticipate, and pray for revival, but we must seek the Lord until he comes in mighty power upon us.

WORDS

Our words are important. Grace is the element in which the believer moves to come into the family of God. "For by grace are ye saved through faith; and that not of yourselves: it is the gift of God: Not of works, lest any man should boast" (Ephesians 2:8, 9, KJV). According to God's mercy he has saved us. *Grace* is that element in the character of God that brings us into his family. We are to talk with grace, Paul said, and our words are to be pleasant. We like to be around people who talk pleasantly. If we make such speech habitual, we will naturally be kind and gracious when we have the opportunity to witness to someone on the outside. We don't become kind and gracious overnight. It takes practice. If we want to give a good witness for Christ, we must practice being kind and gracious so that when we find ourselves under pressure, we will respond in a gracious, pleasant, kind way.

Our words are to be "seasoned with salt" (4:6, KJV). This could mean several things. We know what it means to season food with salt. Salt makes the food taste better by bringing out the flavor. The language of the Christian toward those who are lost ought to create or cultivate an appetite for the gospel because our words are seasoned with salt. The gospel ought to be scintillating, not depressing, sad, or forbidding.

Robert Louis Stevenson went to church one night and wrote in his diary: "I went to church tonight. Strangely to say, I was not greatly depressed." Who said the gospel was supposed to be dull, flat, or insipid? Who said it was supposed to be tasteless and depressing? It ought to be presented as the most exciting adventure story in the world. The most blessed person in the world is one who knows Jesus Christ and lives and walks with him. Our speech ought to reflect that.

The world has not rejected Christianity—it has just rejected the way we describe it. The gospel is unchangeable, but we need to present it in a tasteful, timely way. It should be as attractive and appealing as it was intended to be. We have a hard time selling something that didn't do us any good. Our speech being "seasoned with salt" means that we have appropriated the grace of God, have had an experience with Christ, and share our faith in an appealing, attractive, exciting, and adventuresome way.

Salt is also a preservative. It keeps some things from spoiling. This is a reminder to us that our speech ought not to be corrupt or corrupting. If our language is "seasoned with salt," we will be spared from corruption. God forbid that a professing child of God use filthy language. Speech "seasoned with salt" is pure, never corrupted, spoiled, nor vulgar. The world is not impressed when we as Christians use the same language it uses. There needs to be something distinctly different in the way a Christian talks.

" . . . For then you will have the right answer for everyone" (4:6). If we live as Paul has just described, if we walk in wisdom toward the world, redeem the time, and use speech always seasoned with salt, our manner of life will create opportunities for us to witness. Notice the phrase, "the right *answer* for everyone." If we lived as we ought to, we would not have to look for someone to witness to, for people would be coming to ask us questions about our faith. The very fact that we have to look might indicate that something is wrong!

"Quietly trust yourself to Christ your Lord and if anybody asks why you believe as you do, be ready to tell him, and do it in a gentle and respectful way" (1 Peter 3:15). Peter said earlier, "It is God's will that your good lives should silence those who foolishly condemn the Gospel without knowing what it can do for them, having never experienced its power" (1 Peter 2:15).

There will always be misunderstandings, accusations, but our Christian life-style should help shut them up. The way we live, the way we conduct ourselves toward those outside the faith should stop their criticism and provoke questions about our life-style. Then we should respond with words of grace, "seasoned with salt"—preserving words of God's grace and salvation.

15

Christian
Friends
Colossians
4:7–18

"TYCHICUS, OUR MUCH LOVED BROTHER, will tell you how I am getting along. He is a hard worker and serves the Lord with me. I have sent him on this special trip just to see how you are, and to comfort and encourage you" (4:7, 8).

Many people think that the closing verses of the New Testament epistles are just an expanded way of saying, "Yours truly." But the last verses of Colossians provide some of the most interesting studies in the New Testament. From them we learn much about the personal lives of the people of the early church.

The passage, filled with application, has some very personal touches. Paul spoke of companionship, concern, and consolation, all a part of what Christian friendship means to us.

CHRISTIAN COMPANIONSHIP

Paul listed some of his companions who stood with him: Tychicus, Aristarchus, Mark, Justus, Epaphras, Luke, and Demas. These verses remind us of our tremendous need for other people. None of us was meant to stand alone. If we sometimes feel lonely and burdened with what has been thrust upon us, it may be because we were not intended to bear it alone. God created the family of faith in order for us to share with each other.

We have to be impressed with Paul's list of three Jews and three Gentiles who were especially close to him. They were his companions, his encouragers. They lifted him up and stood by his side. It is possible that one of these may actually have become a prisoner because of his close concern and compassion for the Apostle Paul. Tychicus is called "a fellow servant," which literally means "a fellow slave." Some commentaries suggest that because of his sympathy for Paul, he actually shared his cell as a prisoner in order to be along side of him. It is a beautiful picture of close companionship, of friends sharing one with another.

Tychicus was called "a beloved brother." As such he is related to other Christians. Paul said, "He is one of you." The word "brother" in the Greek language means "from a common source, from a common origin." Paul was saying, "He shares your life and your faith with you."

"He is a brother to you," Paul said. Tychicus was also called "a faithful minister" (KJV). We translate "minister" as "deacon." It speaks of a servant who can be relied upon, of one who longs to minister and serve and who is faithful at the task.

He was also called "a fellow servant" (KJV), which means he had joined with the Apostle Paul in his bondage—if not physically, then spiritually in his heart and with his encouragement. He was a wonderful encourager, partner, and brother, in the ministry of the Lord.

Each of us needs to be that kind of person to another. We need people like that for ourselves. We need to share that spirit of encouragement within the fellowship of the church.

"I am sending Onesimus, a faithful and much loved brother, one of your own people. He and Tychicus will give you all the latest news" (4:9). Onesimus was described in greater detail in the book of Philemon. He was a runaway slave whom Paul had led to Christ. When he got saved, the Apostle Paul sent him back to his master, who was a Christian also. Paul sent him back with instructions to submit to his master. And he sent a note to Philemon, his master, telling him to accept him back as a brother.

It would have been hard to maintain a master-slave relationship under those conditions. Paul did not go into that kind of detail in this passage. But he did call Onesimus "a faithful and beloved brother." He reminded the Colossians that he was one of them; it was a gentle reminder that they were to receive him, not to hold his past against him. They were not to consider him as a slave but as a brother. They were not to look down on him or feel superior to him, but to love him in the Lord and receive him as such.

He sent Onesimus along with Tychicus, who was to deliver the message. Doubtless this friend who went with Onesimus was there to vouch for him. Runaway slaves were often received and returned to servitude, and Philemon might have considered putting Onesimus back into bondage. Paul identified him as a faithful and beloved brother, certainly indicating that Paul considered everyone equal in the family of God.

"Aristarchus, who is with me here as a prisoner, sends you his love, and so does Mark, a relative of Barnabas. And as I said before, give Mark a hearty welcome if he comes your way" (4:10). The Mark referred to was John Mark. It is intriguing that Luke, the beloved physician, and Mark— two of the four Gospel writers—were with the Apostle Paul on his journey to Rome. Imagine the conversation that Mark and Luke must have had together and the things they must have shared! It could explain some of the similarity that exists in their accounts of the life of Christ.

Mark had gone with Paul and Barnabas on their first missionary journey. But he had become discouraged, quit, and gone home. Then when Paul and Barnabas were getting ready to go on the second trip, Barnabas suggested they take along John Mark, but Paul refused. It was hard for Paul to forgive what Mark had done. It took time for him to get over it. As a result, Paul went his way and Barnabas went his.

But here on the final journey of the Apostle Paul to Rome, we find John Mark. He had dropped out for awhile, had made some mistakes, but here he was on this journey to Rome. It is a picture of a man who redeemed himself, a man who made good after he had failed. He had disappointed his friends and turned his back on his commitment, but here he was in those pressure-packed days with Paul in Rome.

The story of John Mark is an encouraging one. We all, at one time or another, need to redeem ourselves. All of us have, at some point, quit and turned our backs on a commitment. All of us have stumbled and fallen. John Mark showed us that a person can redeem himself and come back strong for God. How encouraging that ought to be to us!

Our failure doesn't have to be final. We can come back because the family of God has that kind of forgiveness, warmth, and encouragement to share.

Here was Christian companionship demonstrated by a list of names. It reminds us of our tremendous need for each other, of our need to encourage. Can you imagine where John Mark would have been had Barnabas not put his arm around him and said, "It's all right, John Mark. I believe in you. You go with me. Paul can go with Silas, but I want you to go with me." His encouragement salvaged John Mark for the cause of Christ. Everyone of us can think of someone who once was active in the church but no longer comes. Who will be the Barnabas to go and encourage that person, to help draw him back into the family fellowship? Receiving one another into the family of God is the picture of a deep personal involvement characterized by love, encouragement, and prayer for each other. This is real Christian companionship.

CHRISTIAN CONCERN

"Jesus Justus also sends his love. These are the only Jewish Christians working with me here, and what a comfort they have been! Epaphras, from your city, a servant of Christ Jesus, sends you his love. He is always earnestly praying for you, asking God to make you strong and perfect and to help you know his will in everything you do. I can assure you that he has worked hard for you with his prayers, and also for the Christians in Laodicea and Hierapolis" (4:11–13).

Epaphras was a model of Christian concern. Paul said of him: "He is always earnestly praying for you." "Earnestly praying" is an athletic metaphor. Paul must have loved athletics, for he frequently drew analogies of the Christian life from athletic competition, training, and discipline. This term speaks of tremendous effort, energy, and intense struggle. It is a clear picture of how greatly Epaphras wrestled in prayer for them. Obviously, he didn't just say, "God bless those folks at Colosse." He wrestled in prayer as though he were in spiritual battle. God honors that kind of prayer because of the tremendous concern it demonstrates.

Epaphras prayed " . . . that ye may stand perfect and complete in all the will of God" (4:12, KJV). "Stand" is the word that means "to stand fast," "stand tall," "stand firm," "be solid in your stance." "Perfect and complete" conveys the picture of being fully grown, having achieved everything that is in God's will for us to achieve.

Paul said of him, "I bear him record that he hath great zeal for you" (KJV). The word "great zeal" speaks of toil and labor. The same words are found in the book of Revelation where they carry the idea of pain. When Paul talked about "great zeal," he was talking about a concern deep enough to cause agony and anguish of heart. It says, in effect, "I am praying for you until it hurts. I am laboring for you. I am literally dying for you."

So involved was Paul in Christian concern that it is little wonder that the early church shook the Roman Empire with its life and strength. They had a genuineness and a depth of concern characterized by much prayer. When our concern for one another becomes so great that we pray for each other like that, we can expect the kind of results that Epaphras saw from his prayers. Then we can be to each other what we ought to be, and then God will be able to do great things in and through us.

CHRISTIAN CONSOLATION

"Dear doctor Luke sends his love, and so does Demas. Please give my greetings to the Christian friends at Laodicea, and to Nymphas, and to those who meet in his home" (4:14, 15). Paul referred to the Christians at Laodicea as "brethren" (KJV). Obviously the early churches kept in touch with each other. They frequently exchanged visitors, so they knew what was going on. They also shared a common goal and a common heritage. Since they were about the same business, they were interested in what was happening in other churches. It seems that they circulated the apostles' letters from church to church as well.

Churches in our day seem to have lost some of that sharing. We would sometimes rather think ours is the only church where anything good is happening. We don't want to share in the hurts of other churches or to minister to other churches in their needs. But the early churches certainly did. The only things in our day that approach that are some of the evangelistic crusades when churches share.

Paul sent greetings also to "Nymphas and the church which is in his house" (KJV). Depending on the translation, it may say, "her house" because the Greek language is unclear as to whether the noun is masculine or feminine. The important point is that there was a church meeting in a house. Remember that the early church didn't have buildings. It was years before they erected special buildings for meeting places. The early churches usually met in people's homes.

The physical buildings are not the essential factor of the church. We need physical buildings, and we want to have the best we can, but the building is not the church. The church is a living organism composed of people; the meeting place is just a matter of convenience. Someone described it: "The church is never a place but a people; never a fold, but a flock; never a sacred building, but a believing assembly."

The church is wherever we are. Sometimes we act different in the church than we do on the job or at school or at home. However, if we believe that people are the essential factor, then wherever the people are, there is the church.

Paul added, "By the way, after you have read this letter . . ." (4:16). The verb "to read" means "to read aloud." It was the common word used for reading in the synagogue. The Word of God was read aloud in the early church after the pattern in the Jewish synagogue.

"And say to Archippus, 'Be sure that you do all the Lord has told you to do' " (4:17). Some have wondered why Paul told Archippus, "Take heed to the ministry which thou hast received in the Lord, that thou fulfill it" (KJV). It is clear that Paul was not rebuking him, for it was not like Paul to single one person out for public embarrassment. Had he wanted to speak to him about some laxity or laziness or to encourage him to be diligent and work hard, then Paul would have written to him privately.

It is possible that Archippus was a young man who had been chosen, at least on an interim basis, to be the pastor of the church. Paul was saying to him, "Take heed to the ministry, God gave it to you. God put you where you are. So give diligence to it. Do your best to let God use you in a very special way." It seems Paul intended his remark to encourage Archippus to follow through on the task that God had given to him.

Then Paul said, "Here is my greeting in my own handwriting." We recall from 2 Thessalonians that a forged letter had been circulated. Someone claiming to be Paul had written a letter which caused a lot of problems. Paul always had a scribe to write the letters for him, but he would sign it in his own handwriting. That is why he pointed out that the greeting was in his signature.

"Remember my bonds" (KJV). This concluding thought is a very tender, pathetic touch. It may be equal to his saying, "Remember me in prayer." It had to be a very touching thing for them, for he was saying, "Just remember, I love you and care for you very much. I am in prison because of my commitment to Jesus Christ. And the perils of false doctrines that have assailed you as a church cause great anxiety for me in my bonds. How I want to be with you and share with you and to give you the truth without any mixture of compromise! Remember me in my bonds."

"Grace be with you" (KJV). That was a tender and specific way of acknowledging the bond between them. In reading this closing benediction, we are reminded again how much we need each other's encouragement and support. As a church we need to be strong in our labor for the Lord. How can the church be strong? By individually being what God wants us to be. Then we will truly be the family, the Church, the living Body of Christ, the portrait of Christ made manifest in the world, as God intends for us to be.